# SECRET
# WHITECHAPEL

## Louis Berk & Rachel Kolsky

AMBERLEY

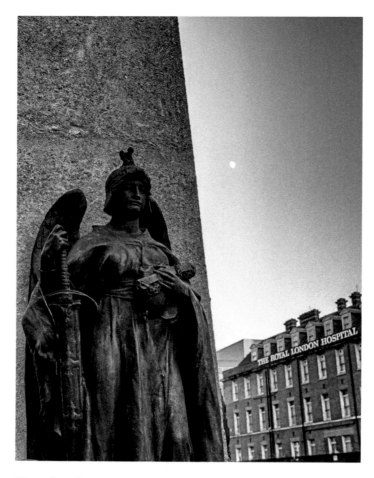

King Edward VII Memorial Fountain.

First published 2017

Amberley Publishing
The Hill, Stroud, Gloucestershire, GL5 4EP
www.amberley-books.com

Copyright © Louis Berk & Rachel Kolsky, 2017

The right of Louis Berk & Rachel Kolsky to be
identified as the Authors of this work has been
asserted in accordance with the Copyrights, Designs
and Patents Act 1988.

ISBN  978 1 4456 6198 8 (print)
ISBN  978-1-4456 6199 5 (ebook)

British Library Cataloguing in Publication Data.
A catalogue record for this book is available from the
British Library.

Origination by Amberley Publishing.
Printed in Great Britain.

# Contents

Map                                        4

Key                                        5

Welcome to Secret Whitechapel              6

Secret Whitechapel                         9

About the Authors                         93

Acknowledgements                          94

Locations                                 95

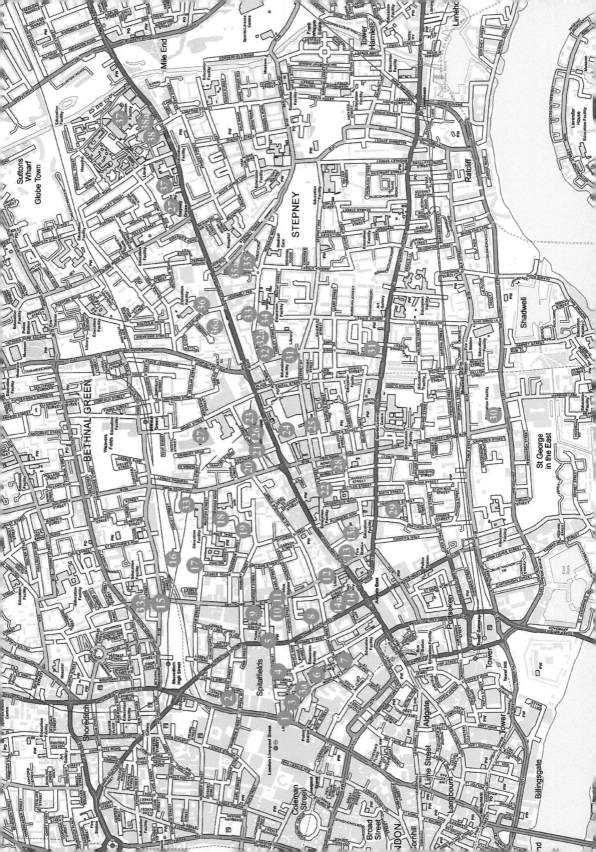

# KEY

1. Battle of the Books
2. Step Back in Time at Dennis Severs' House
3. Ye Olde England
3a. Façadsim
4. Ghost Signs of Spitalfields
5. Going Bananas!
6. The Parliament of Petticoat Lane
7. Merchant House
8. The First 4 Per Cent Buildings
9. The Man Who Became a Room
10. Looking Up
11. History at Your Feet
12. Bohemian Rhapsody in Osborn Street
13. Changes at Itchy Park
13a. St Boniface
14. Anarchist Faces
14a. *Jewish Daily Post*
15. Street Signs
16. Underneath the Arches
17. The Spitalfields Gourd
18. Mother Levy's
19. Light Is My Glory
20. Hopetown

21. The Revolutionary Door in Fulbourne Street
22. Plotting and Protesting
23. Angels and Cherubs
24. 'The London'
25. Alexandra: 'The London's Princess'
26. The Penny Gaff and The Elephant Man
27. An Oasis in Whitechapel
28. Academy to Army
29. Tommy Flowers
30. The Mortuary That Became a Nature Study Centre
31. The Siege of Sidney Street
32. The Father of Bangladesh
32a. Remembering the Blitz
33. Challahs to Crodoughs
33a. The Brick Lane Beigel Bake
34. Mercers' Maidens
35. A Nest of Gentle Anarchists
35a. Best for Health
36. Whitechapel Hideaways
36a. Tower Hamlets Mission
37. The House of Life
38. The People's Palace
38a. Four Queens

## How to Use This Book

The map enables you to find the buildings and sites mentioned in the book as the key uses the same numbers as the text. Where there are two numbers the same, they refer to the same entry. Full address details, and websites when appropriate, are listed at the back of the book (*see* Locations). Information regarding transport and websites was correct at time of writing. Transport for London (tfl.gov.uk) is an excellent resource for planning journeys, and before visiting any of the buildings it is advisable to check their websites for opening hours and access.

# Welcome to Secret Whitechapel

Taking a walk eastwards along the wide boulevard Whitechapel Road, at the junction of Cambridge Heath Road it becomes Mile End Road. Very shortly, on the left-hand side you see a colourful mural painted by artist Mychael Barratt. Commissioned by resident law firm T. V. Edwards, it tells the history of Whitechapel through people, buildings and artefacts spanning over 350 years.

Captain Cook, Gandhi, the Queen, Lenin and William Booth mingle with dock cranes and the Liberty Bell cast at the Whitechapel Bell Foundry and shipped to the USA. Indeed, if you study the mural (and we encourage you to do it in person rather than just in this book), it reveals a wonderful cornucopia of connections to famous people and events linked to the history of Whitechapel, many of which are featured in this book.

Our first book for Amberley, *Whitechapel in 50 Buildings*, celebrated buildings that proclaimed from the exterior their age, history or purpose. *Secret Whitechapel* is intended to encourage readers to look up and to look down, discovering stories not immediately evident to the passer-by.

The story of Whitechapel is not always emblazoned on walls but there are often other clues to its fascinating past – they just need interpreting. When passing the Royal London Hospital, you might notice the distinctively shaped windows of the top floor. What do they mean? You can pass by a shopfront on Whitechapel Road without knowing it contained a peep show connected to one of the most moving human stories in English history. Within this book, doors, windows, pavements and even drainpipes – among other items – all have a hidden story to tell.

Whitechapel continues to captivate people from all over the Britain – indeed the world. Many have passed through on their journeys, either living or working there. Within this small area, you discover a microcosm of London's social history and those who strove for change including the Dancing Academy on New Street that hosted missionary meetings that led to an international philanthropic movement. One of the most popular songs of the twentieth century was created in a modest recording studio on Osborn Street and shopfronts and ghost signs are reminders of both past businesses and those now in fourth-generation family ownership.

In between, the fabric of Whitechapel has been greatly influenced by successive waves of immigrants who have also left their mark on the area. From the Jewish community comes the memoir of a young man encountering the dank foreboding tunnel linking one side of Whitechapel with the other, and from the recent wave of Bangladeshi immigrants comes the creation of a magical farm growing exotic produce.

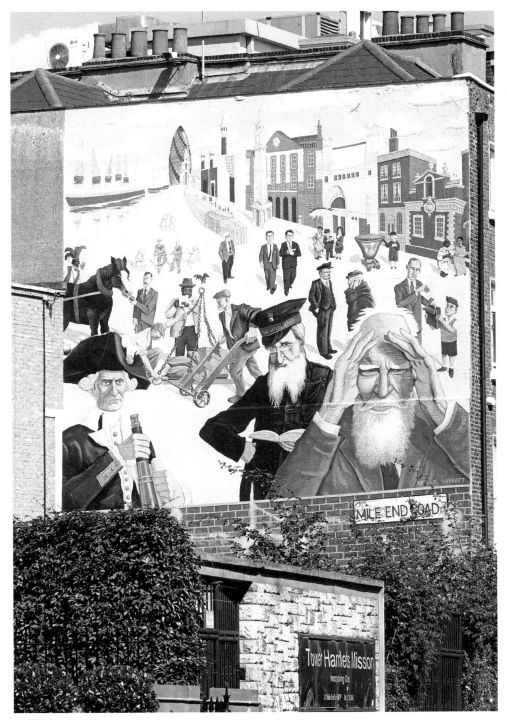

Mile End mural at No. 31 Mile End Road, E1. (Courtesy of artist Mychael Barratt, commissioned by T. V. Edwards)

It would be impossible to reveal all the secrets within Whitechapel in one single volume. Indeed, as we wrote this book we continued to discover more wonderful stories that for reasons of space we had to omit. If we had to sum up this collection of special places, we chose to concentrate on the minutiae and truly hidden meanings in buildings and locations. There is a vicarious delight in knowing you are following in the footsteps of famous men and women in history, or finding spaces that, even in Whitechapel, are so 'off the beaten track' they appear almost rural.

There is no doubt that Whitechapel is going through an important transition as the thirst for space pushes outwards from the nearby City of London. Central Whitechapel is likely to go through dramatic changes during the rest of this decade as Crossrail arrives and the London Borough of Tower Hamlets commences its vision for a new twenty-first-century civic centre for its borough. There may yet be time to savour some of the back roads and surprisingly tranquil spaces shown in this book and we hope it will both inform and fulfil its role as a guide to secrets in the area.

*Louis Berk and Rachel Kolsky, September 2017*

# Secret Whitechapel

## 1. Battle of the Books

The Bishopsgate Institute Library is found within the Bishopsgate Institute, opened by Lord Rosebery in 1895. The institute was funded by the amalgamation of several small charities in the local parish with the aim 'to promote lectures, exhibitions and otherwise the advancement of literature, science and fine arts'.

It included a Great Hall, holding up to 500 people, and reference and lending libraries. While the first-floor reading room is now no longer a library, the ground floor remains a gem of a reference library complete with walls lined with wooden bookshelves, many of them with lockable glass doors.

Welcomed by librarians at the central information desk, visitors' eyes are taken by the beautiful white and yellow glass cupola above the reading desks. Bringing in extra light, essential to the original readers, it survived the Second World War intact having been wrapped up in padding. The original bookplates were designed by Walter Crane and as the book collection expanded, the Library was extended in 1911. An extensive renovation in 1997 restored the original colour scheme.

Today the collection provides directories, quick reference works and press cuttings mostly linked to London's social history and, in particular, the East End. Special London collections include those of social workers Doris and Muriel Lester, humanist Charles Bradlaugh, historian Raphael Samuel and the Co-operative movement. The photo archive is vast providing a unique insight into the local area, including many of the sites profiled in this book. The whole room emits the unique memories of over a century of inquisitive readers in the search for knowledge and enlightenment.

However, the tranquillity of the library belies controversies of the past. In 1897 Charles Goss arrived as librarian, not leaving until 1941 when he was ousted over the Battle of the Books. Quirky, precise and with a magnificent moustache curling beyond his cheeks, Charles was also, in many ways, the quintessential librarian, acquiring books and cataloguing them with care and reverence. He implemented systems to indicate if books were available or not and it was his insistence on closed access that proved his downfall. He believed open access encouraged theft and that readers did not benefit from browsing the bookshelves themselves and that they should use his catalogue. With Charles's refusal to adapt, the interwar years saw lending library visitors diminish and his beloved Cotgreave Indicator became a curiosity rather than a regular working tool. During the Second World War, he was removed from the post and it is said that he never returned to the library again.

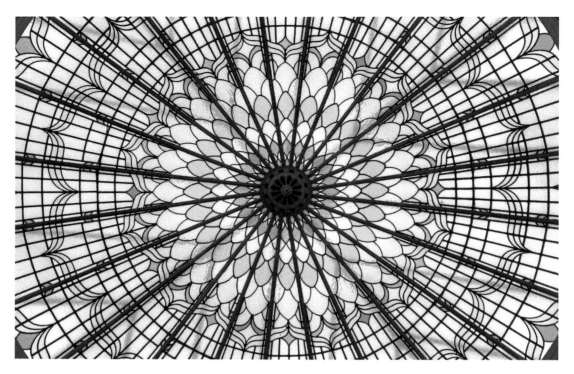

The Bishopsgate Institute Library. (Photo: Richard Kearns. © The Bishopsgate Institute)

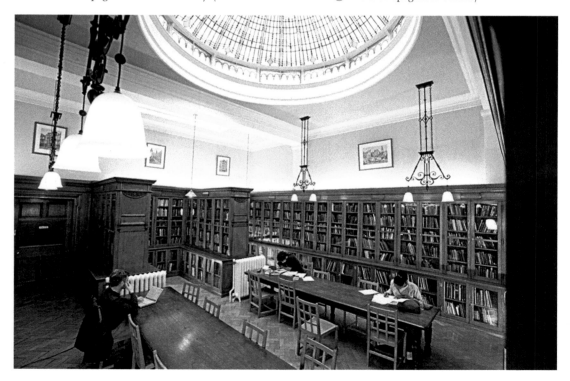

Post-war, Charles's closed access system was ended, the first-floor reading room was turned into a restaurant, later closing in 1985, and the library became reference only. With no new special collections arriving for over seventy-five years, there was a renaissance in the late twentieth century when several arrived in quick succession and the library re-established itself as central to those living and working in the area.

Charles Goss did leave a lasting legacy in the form of photos taken in 1910 when he ventured out onto Bishopsgate and captured the everyday scenes around him. They complement perfectly those taken just two years later by C. A. Mathews (*see* entry No. 3) which are also held at this library.

## 2. Step Back in Time at Dennis Severs' House

At the northern end of Folgate Street, a row of eighteenth-century houses still stand almost in defiance of the gradual 'creep' of steel and glass of City tower blocks into Norton Folgate at the end of the street. No. 18 has brightly coloured paintwork and shutters of black and red with a gaslight above the front door. At first glance, it is indistinguishable from its neighbours but looking more closely there are silhouettes of a gentleman and lady at the windowpanes and an outline of a canary in a cage.

This is Dennis Severs' House and the relatively unadorned exterior does not prepare visitors for the glorious experience that awaits them as they step back in time to a capsule of eighteenth- and nineteenth-century London, taking you from the wealth of a silk merchants' dining room of the 1720s to a parlour of the days of the First World War.

Californian-born Dennis Severs visited London in 1965 as a teenager and gripped by the history, he returned as a young man, trained as a barrister but became a tour guide, transporting his visitors around the city in a horse and carriage. As an 'outsider', he found the Spitalfields of the late 1970s welcoming and non-judgemental. In 1979, he bought what was then a rundown house in an area characterised by decay and peopled with down and outs huddled around the warming braziers. Spitalfields Market was still selling fruits and vegetables and each day began in the early hours of the morning, when the narrow streets and loading bays were filled with lorries and fresh produce. Few people actually lived there. Dennis did not know it but he was a pioneer, recognising the special spirit of the space. His arrival coincided with kindred spirits – the area was attracting interest of those keen to preserve this corner of Georgian London – Raphael Samuel, the historian lived in Elder Street where Dan Cruikshank and his supporters had squatted in the houses to prevent demolition, and the artist colony was beginning to take shape following the recent arrival of modern artists Gilbert and George, who lived close by (and still do) in Fournier Street.

He slept in each of the ten rooms of his new home and gradually his imagined story of the French Huguenot Gervais family took root. He furnished each room to reveal a different period in the family history. Their story incorporated social changes such marrying out of the Huguenot faith and the Anglicisation of the name to Jervis. Artisans and artists commissioned by Dennis entered enthusiastically into his venture and with humour. They were instructed that nothing contemporary was allowed but the ceramicist for the Delft fireplace cleverly incorporated figures of Gilbert and George into one of the

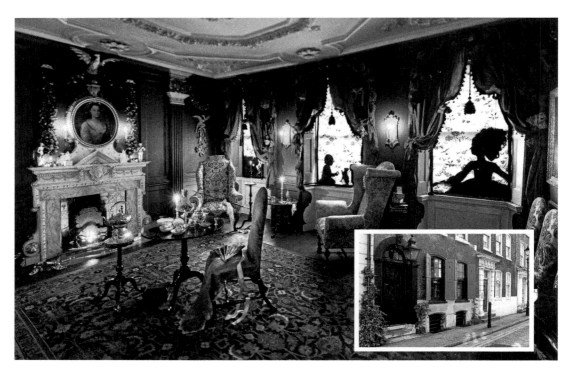

Dennis Severs' House. (© Dennis Severs' House)

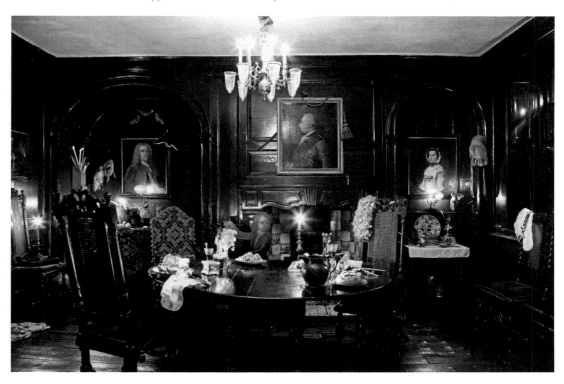

tiles. Sound effects were added giving a sense of conversation, whispers and laughter and even the clip-clop of the horses' hoofs taking imaginary visitors away. Chairs fallen on their backs enticed thoughts of those who had left the room in haste and why, glasses of port brought to mind a gentlemen's postprandial drinks and details such as a wig on a chair-back completed the illusion.

Dennis opened his home to the public welcoming visitors when they entered into the spirit of his endeavour, exploring in silence and breathing in the aura. 'You either see it or you don't' he would say, and those who sought to catch him out by looking for a telephone or signs of twentieth-century living were summarily removed from the premises! The highlight of each year remains Christmastime when No. 18 is additionally decorated with sweetmeats and orange pomanders and the aroma of spiced mulled wine permeates throughout the house. Sadly, Dennis died in 1999. He left copious instructions regarding maintenance and public access. Today, his home remains a popular attraction evoking the lost world of Spitalfields when it was the centre of the silk trade and the houses had not yet been transformed into East End tailoring workshops and slum homes. Importantly, the house is a lasting legacy to a visionary who reinvented history as an experience for all the senses.

# 3. Ye Olde England

Artillery Passage with its picturesque hanging signs evoking 'ye olde England' is perhaps one of London's most photographed alleyways. Connecting Sandys Row to Artillery Lane near Spitalfields Market, the recent transformation of this narrow pedestrian thoroughfare from a down at heel row of shops to one filled with eateries, including the esteemed Ottolenghi restaurant, bespoke tailoring and a parfumier is a metaphor for the regeneration of Spitalfields itself.

The land, originally part of the Priory of St Mary Spital, a religious house founded in 1197, included a hospital, graveyard, charnel house and residential buildings. Appropriated in 1537 by Henry VIII during the Dissolution of the Monasteries, it was designated an artillery ground for use of 'longbowes, crossbowes and handegonnes'.

In 1682, the land was sold to George Bradbury and Edward Noell and their new development included the street names Artillery Passage, Artillery Lane and Fort and Gun Streets commemorating its past use.

Huguenots, French Protestants fleeing persecution in the 1690s, were among the first residents. Parliament Court, a narrow alley off Artillery Passage where a French church was established, is named from 'parler', the French word for to talk. The Irish followed and then the Jewish immigrants, firstly from northern Europe and then later Russia and Poland. Businesses ranged from silk weaving to tailoring workshops, hardware stores and hairdressers.

C. A. Mathews' photographs taken on 20 April 1912 captured several shopfronts cornering Artillery Passage. At the northern end was 'Woolf, Dealer in All Kinds' and at the south was a tobacconist where the Titanic tragedy still dominated newspaper headlines. By the late twentieth century, the area was dominated by premises linked to the declining garment

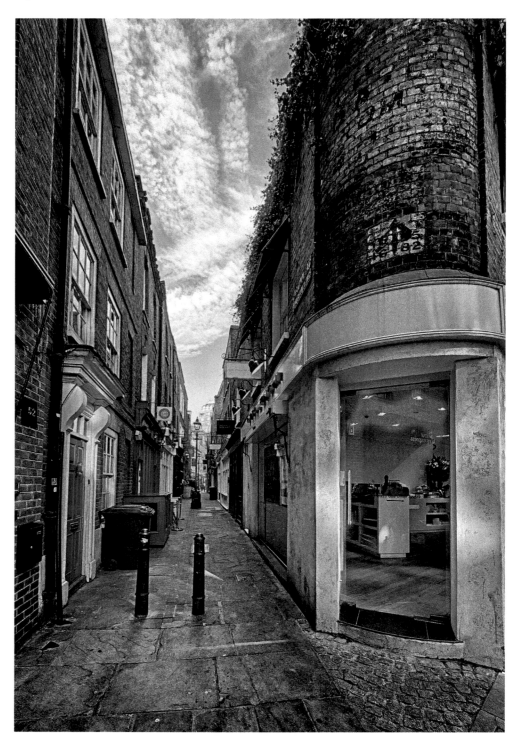

Artillery Passage.

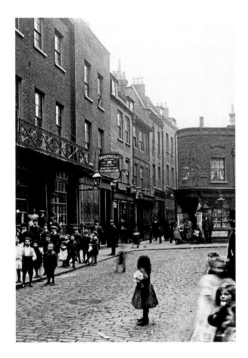 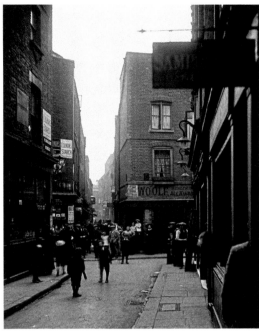

Artillery Passage, 1912. (Courtesy The Bishopsgate Institute)

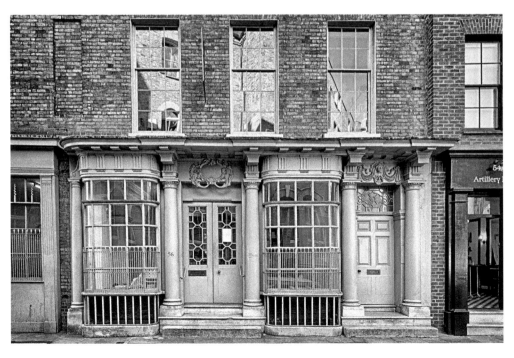

Raven Row.

trade and local market traders and following the departure of Spitalfields Market, the streets with their Georgian shop frontages, mostly intact, gradually reinvented themselves.

Emerging from the southern end of the Passage into Artillery Lane, on the left-hand corner is a plaque commemorating 1682 and on the right-hand side are two beautifully curved front windows. They lead to Raven Row, a contemporary not-for-profit art gallery showcasing upcoming artists who might otherwise not be exhibited. It is named after the portion of Artillery Lane known by that name until 1895. The gallery opened in 2009 after extensive restoration of two houses, Nos 56 and 58. Dating from the 1690s, the buildings were remodelled in the 1750s for Huguenot silk merchants. The windows at No. 56 installed in 1767 remain some of the oldest shopfronts in London complete with Doric columns and a lozenge above the door. Later use of the site included a grocer and Jewish garment workshops but by the late 1990s it was empty and in decay. Alex Sainsbury, of the supermarket dynasty, bought the property in 2004 and his careful restoration retains the elaborate rococo detail but also inserted two new galleries in the basement. There was a surprise to come his way. The flat on the fourth floor of No. 56 was inhabited by Rebecca Levy. She had moved into the building with her family in 1918 and by 2004 was the sole survivor. Alex allowed her to remain and only when she passed away in 2009, aged ninety-eight, was the flat incorporated as gallery space.

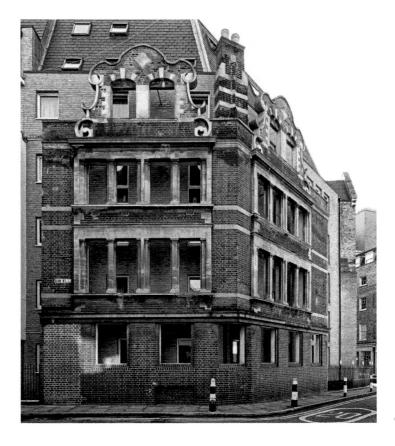

Gun Street Double Wall.

**DID YOU KNOW?**

A piece of the original back elevation of Providence Row, a refuge for the homeless, between Artillery Lane and Gun Street, is linked with metal brackets to the newly built accommodation for LSE students. In the UK, where redundant buildings are redeveloped for new use, a part of the original structure is often saved and attached to the new structure. Dubbed 'façadism' by architectural critics, reactions are mixed but here in Spitalfields, this example always catches the eye of visitors emerging from Artillery Passage.

# 4. The Ghost Signs of Spitalfields

Brick walls are perfect canvases for large outdoor advertisements. Back in the day useful incomes were made from owners renting out their walls to companies willing to pay for sign writers to adorn them with advertising slogans. If you owned the wall yourself, so much the better.

At the corner of Crispin and Brushfield Streets two signs survive, Donovan Bros, bag makers, and Percy Dalton, peanut roaster. These Spitalfields Market businesses remain going concerns having relocated elsewhere and have not suffered the fate of so many of the other local businesses that closed down when the market relocated to Leyton in 1991. They are also reminders, not only of businesses integral to the bustling Spitalfields Market, but also two immigrant communities, the Irish and Jewish.

Donovan Bros with their recently repainted sign looking very dapper in stylish green and ochre, proclaims itself as 'The Noted House for Paper Bags'. Jeremiah O'Donovan arrived in London during the 1830s and settled in Aldgate. It was a Patrick Donovan, the 'O' having been lost along the way, who established the business and with eight siblings, there were Donovan paper bag branches at all London's wholesale markets. In the 1960s, their shop on Commercial Street listed branches at Borough, Stratford and Deptford but they also had a presence at Covent Garden. Now headquartered at Sidcup, Donovans still operate at London's wholesale markets but they have diversified from paper bags and florist tissue paper to an online cornucopia of bags, biodegradable tableware, labels and boxes. Other memories return too: buying a pound of apples with the stallholder spinning the brown paper bag making 'ears' from the corners, and the local Irish community itself often forgotten in an area dominated by memories of the Jewish East End.

Associated mainly with the tailoring trade, there were many Jewish traders at Spitalfields. Some were wholesalers such as the Mekelburgs, who traded as M. Mack from the 1920s, and Ivor Robins, who became Master of the Worshipful Company of Fruiterers. Others were secondary wholesalers like David Kira (*see* entry No. 5) whose clients were market traders and high street greengrocers. Percy Dalton traded fruit and imported nuts in the 1930s and utilised the backyard of his premises for roasting monkey nuts in their shells. Sold in small paper bags that instructed they could only be used to sell Percy

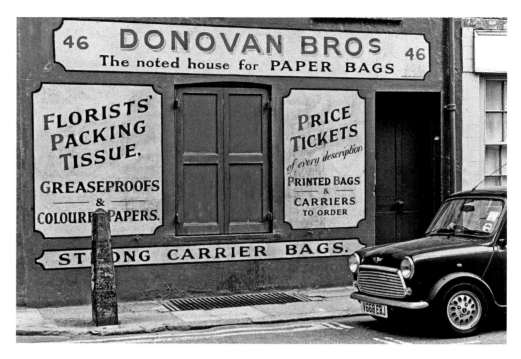

Donovan Bros.

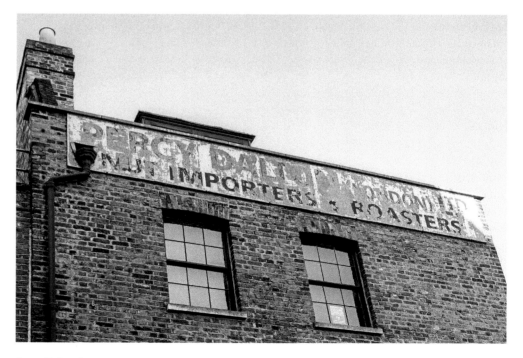

Percy Dalton's.

Dalton nuts, they became ubiquitous and a byword for the tastiest peanuts. The sign, now very weathered, is painted on a metal sheet affixed by hooks to the bricks. After moving from Spitalfields to Fish Island, Hackney, Percy Dalton moved again in 2005 to Suffolk and the Hackney peanut factory became a complex of artists' studios.

The signs have one further link, although it is not immediately evident. They were both painted by commercial artist Alfred Keil, whose signage business was around the corner at Whites Row between the 1930s and 1950s. However, not everything is as it seems. The green and ochre Donovan Bros advert incorporates the signature 'Alfred Keil Signs BIS 4169', as a form of self-advertising. Alphabetical telephone exchanges (the BIS stood for Bishopsgate) were discontinued in 1968 and at that time the Donovan design at Crispin Street was bright red and yellow and continued to be so until at least the mid-1980s. Could it be that when Alfred devised the new colour scheme for Donovan he could not resist incorporating a piece of Spitalfields design heritage? In doing so, he reminds everyone of the unsung heroes of signage (*see* entry No. 35).

# 5. Going Bananas!

When exploring London's urban landscape one can sometimes find totally incongruous signage. For instance, the fascia of a hairdressing salon in Fournier Street proclaims the name 'David Kira' above its premises. To anyone familiar with Spitalfields, David Kira Ltd was a familiar landmark at No. 1 Fournier Street, being the premises of the market's foremost banana merchant until 1991 when the market relocated. Amazingly, the businesses that have traded here since, have retained the interior with minimal intervention.

This is a story of bananas and it began with Sam Kira in Southend, a Jewish immigrant from Poland who became naturalised in 1929 and started a company called El Dorado Bananas. Ten years later, his son, David, opened up in Fournier Street as a wholesaler, taking a lease from Lady Fox but having to leave the business almost at once when the Second World War began, bringing conscription and wiping out the banana trade. A letter from the Fox Estate to David Kira in 1941 states that,

> whilst the present ban on the importation of bananas into this country remains in force, or you are otherwise prevented from carrying on business, our client will accept a reduced rental of £100 per annum in respect of the lease of these premises. It is of course understood that this is a temporary arrangement only to assist you in your difficulty and the position must be reviewed from time to time.

The importation of bananas resumed in 1946 and David built a loyal clientele and an enviable reputation.

David purchased the freehold of both No 1 and No 3 Fournier Street from the trustees of Lady Fox in 1953 for the total sum of £4,230. His son, Stuart, joined him in 1962 and with their loyal partner John Neil, cashier Ted Witt, two porters, Alf Lee and Billy Alloway, and an 'empty boy' who collected and stacked empty wooden fruit boxes, the team was complete.

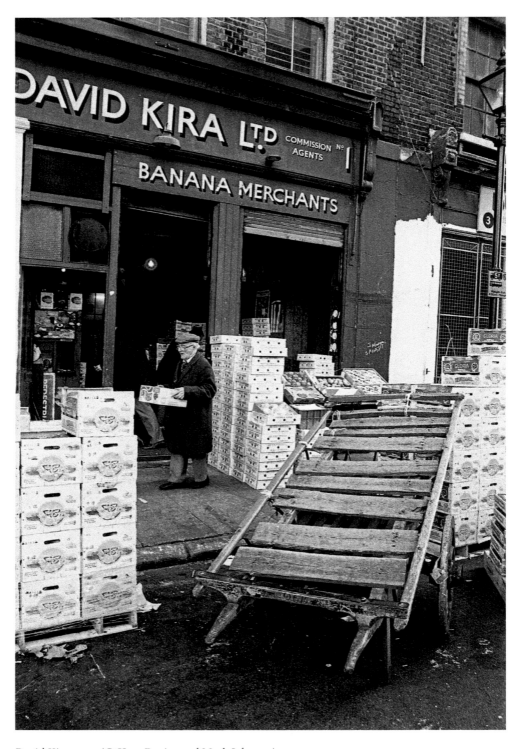

David Kira, 1991. (© Huw Davies and Mark Johnson)

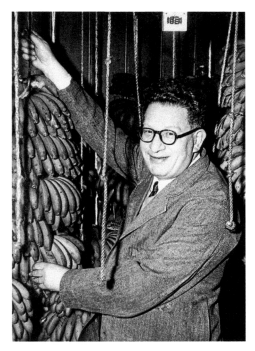 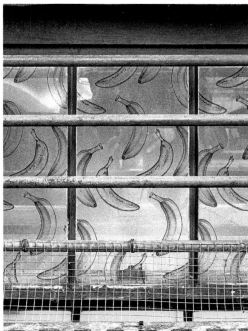

*Above left*: David Kira in the banana storage room. (Courtesy of Stuart Kira)

*Above right*: Bananas, through the windows of the ripening room.

*Below*: Fournier Street in the 1980s, including David Kira. (Courtesy of Stuart Kira)

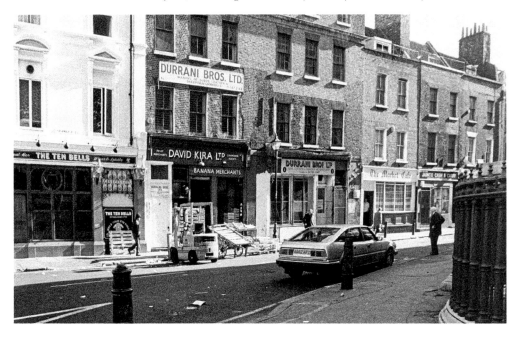

Jamaican bananas arrived directly from the docks, still green and on long stalks, packed in straw. They were unloaded from the lorries promptly, as 'the enemy of the banana is cold' remembers Stuart Kira. The ripening rooms were downstairs and it took five days from arrival until they were saleable. The heat of the Caribbean was emulated in the basements with ethylene lamps in each corner, prompting the name 'Ethel' for Kira's rat-catching cat. A key skill of the trade was holding a stalk of bananas between your legs and cutting off each bunch with a knife and placing the fruit in specially shaped and sized boxes known as 'coffins'.

From the 1980s, bananas were imported pre-boxed and the ripening basements were made redundant. Since the departure of the bananas, the premises were used by a garment business and an upmarket shoe retailer before becoming a hairdresser.

However, David Kira is not just commemorated by the name above the door but also the recently painted bananas behind the basement windows leading to the memories of the ripening floors, Ethel and the spiders that were famously transported in the crates with the fruit. Urban myths abound about local youngsters collecting these creepy crawlies and selling them on as pet food!

## 6. The Parliament of Petticoat Lane, as Remembered by Berk and Berkoff

In 2004, when I first began my ramblings through the back streets of Whitechapel I would walk down Wentworth Street, part of the Petticoat Lane market, and my eyes would be drawn to the pair of public conveniences at the junction with Leyden Street.

Opened in 1900, they are prime examples of late Victorian conveniences and worthy of closer attention. I was particularly intrigued as to why the signs for Ladies and Gentlemen required punctuation and no one has ever been able to adequately explain this to me.

The beautiful cast-iron railings, the stairs that descend into mysterious interiors and the prosaic signage, accompanied by the modern imperative of 'No Dumping', still make me smile when I pass them today.

In my research, I came across the wonderful reminiscences by a famous son of Whitechapel, Steven Berkoff, of his early life there in the 1950s. Apart from acting and writing, he is also an excellent photographer. I'm not sure where I read his account but one which I immediately recognised was his description of 'The Parliament of Petticoat Lane'.

As nature took its course, the mainly Jewish traders of Petticoat Lane at the time would have recourse to use the toilets. As they congregated they would discuss and solve the world's various problems. One can imagine this led to quite heated debate, probably not dissimilar to the activities on the floor of the House of Commons at Westminster, hence the name.

Sadly, today's traders are unable to congregate here as the toilets were closed by the local authority some years ago. They await infill with concrete as they fail to meet specifications laid down by bureaucrats in Brussels who have no soul, or, it would seem, urgent needs. (*Louis Berk*)

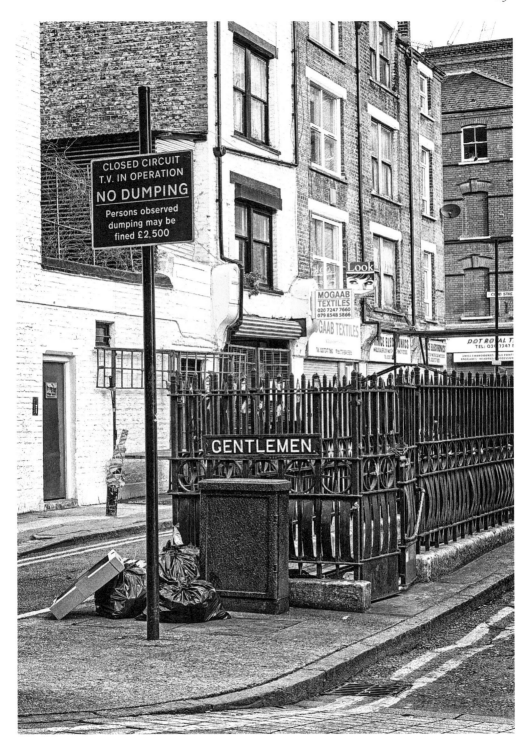

Parliament of Petticoat Lane.

# 7. The Merchant House

Merchant House is part of the Wentworth Dwellings, one of the blocks of social housing funded and erected by the East End Dwelling Co., founded in 1882 by Samuel Barnett, vicar of St Judes's, Commercial Street. He had been inspired by the passing of the Cross Act in 1875 (*see* also entries 8 and 35) when slums were cleared by local authorities but new housing was to be built by private enterprise.

Two adjacent plots were acquired on Goulston Street for the sum of £87,000, which may seem a lot but the actual cost of the purchase and clearance work by the Metropolitan Board of Works had been over £300,000. Such was the concern for the speedy improvement of housing conditions that the loss was not an issue to the authorities.

Brunswick Buildings and Wentworth Dwellings were on Goulston Street, although the entrance to the latter was around the corner on Wentworth Street, now bearing the name Merchant House. Apart from cement pediments displaying the names, the buildings were entirely devoid of ornamentation and despite the apartments sharing communal toilet and laundry facilities, such accommodation was luxurious for the time.

Both blocks survive today and remained social housing until the late twentieth century. They have recently been redeveloped as private housing where, at the time of writing, a one-bedroom home commands a price of over £400,000.

A sinister association with the Whitechapel Murders (the so-called Jack the Ripper murders) of 1888 occurred on the night of 30 September at Wentworth Dwellings. The body of Catherine Eddowes had been found in the early hours of the morning in nearby Mitre Square. During the subsequent search for the perpetrator a policeman found, at 3 a.m., a piece of bloodstained cloth in a narrow arch that led into the buildings from Goulston Street. Thinking it must be where the murderer stopped to wipe his knife, the officer summoned his superiors.

Above the spot where the bloody cloth was discovered was scrawled a puzzling message: 'The Juwes are the men who will not be blamed for nothing.' The exact meaning of this phrase and its association to the cloth has since been the subject of debate by both eminent historians and enthusiastic 'Ripperologists'.

One reason is the reaction of Sir Charles Warren, the Metropolitan Police Commissioner, who ordered its immediate removal. It was initially felt that Warren was taking steps to avoid a confrontation between the gentile and Jewish populations as several Jewish suspects had been interviewed by the police and their identities had been announced in newspaper articles.

However, there is no dispute that the word was 'Juwes' and not 'Jews' and that otherwise the spelling of the rest of the phrase is perfect. Why would this one well-known word have been misspelled? One interpretation, still debated, is that the word 'Juwes' is not a misspelling but is a masonic reference and Warren, a senior Freemason, had it removed to protect other masons.

In 1884, the Barnett's completed College Buildings on Wentworth Street. Using their architect Elijah Hoole, who had designed their settlement Toynbee Hall, this time they allowed their social housing to incorporate a mixture of Victorian Gothic ornamentation and decoration in the Arts and Crafts style.

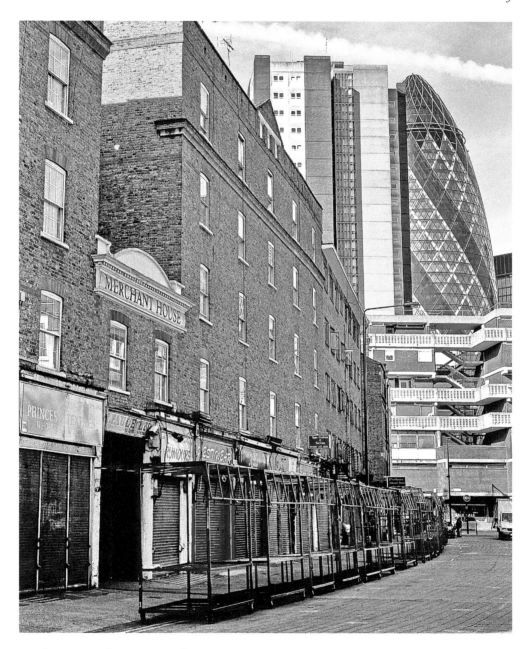

Merchant House from Wentworth Street.

This façade still remains, although the building itself was gutted and modernised in the 1970s. Following its recent demolition, the frontage was retained to be incorporated into a twenty-first-century housing and commercial development being built on the former Toynbee Hall estate.

The Barnett's were part of a group of philanthropists of the time who believed that living conditions and education were key to reducing poverty and improving social mobility. Their initiatives have left a legacy of well-built social housing which stands as an important reminder today of the standards that are required.

## 8. The First 4 Per Cent Buildings

A red-brick arch on Wentworth Street is all that remains of the Charlotte de Rothschild Dwellings. Erected in 1886, it was the first block of flats built by the 4 Per Cent Industrial Dwellings Co., whose name is engraved in the stonework. Now leading to a small estate of low-rise 1980s housing, the story begins in the mid-1880s.

By the late nineteenth century, the population of London was growing fast, particularly in the East End where local industry including the docks provided opportunity for work. Jewish migrants from Russia and Poland swelled the numbers, choosing to join the well-established Jewish community of Whitechapel. Housing was in short supply and many people lived in poverty-stricken rookeries and slums. The Artisans' and Labourers' Dwellings Improvement Act of 1875, known as the Cross Act after the Home Secretary, Richard Cross, allowed for homes to be designated as unfit for habitation, then bought by local authorities and sold to private concerns or philanthropists who would then demolish and rebuild at no cost to the ratepayers. George Peabody had led the way in 1862 with his Peabody Buildings and from 1875 many followed him including the East End Dwellings Co., founded by Samuel Barnett in 1882 (see entry No. 35), and the Guinness Trust in 1890.

Another pioneer was Nathaniel, Lord Rothschild, ennobled in 1885, who encouraged his friends to invest in his initiative to provide affordable housing for the Jewish industrious classes. The financial return would be 4 per cent, hence the name.

This first block, named after his mother, Charlotte, was built in yellow stock brick with little ornamentation, surrounding a courtyard used for drying washing and as a children's playground. Six storeys high, they were quite forbidding and known locally as 'The Buildings'. The first residents arrived in 1887 and eventually it was home to 186 families, mainly, but not exclusively, Jewish.

With running water on all floors and affordable rents, they were an immediate success and workshops originally on the top floors were soon converted into additional flats. The 'Super' (superintendent) vetted all the applicants, reported misconduct and ensured all the rules were kept. Rotas ensured stairwells were swept and steps whitened. The occupations of the first residents were dominated by tailoring followed by the other key Jewish trades of tobacco, furniture, shoe and hat making.

Additional 4 Per Cent blocks soon followed with Brady (1890) in Brady Street, Nathaniel (1892) opposite Charlotte in Wentworth Street and Stepney Green Dwellings (1896) further east at Stepney Green. By 1901, 4,600 people were housed by the 4 Per Cent but of the original four blocks only Stepney Green Dwellings (now Court) remains.

Further north in Dalston the 4 Per Cent built Navarino Mansions, a grand block of mostly one-bedroom dwellings that remains social housing. Mocatta House, much

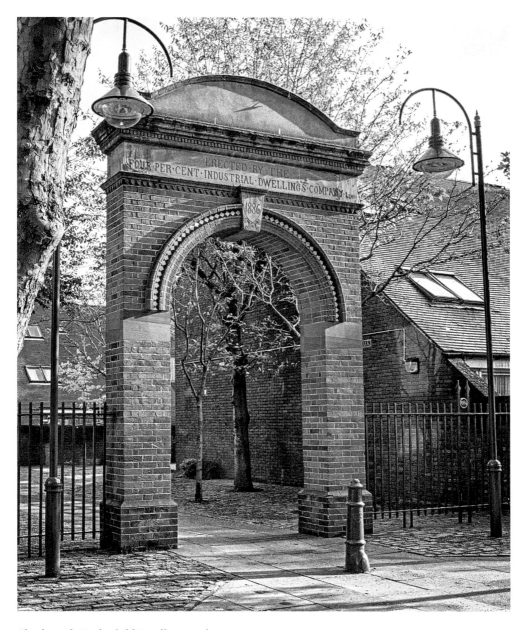

Charlotte de Rothschild Dwellings arch.

smaller currently with just twenty flats, opened on Brady Street in 1905, the last built in Whitechapel by the 4 Per Cent.

The Charlotte de Rothschild Dwellings remained in use until the 1960s, but by then the cost for the London Borough of Tower Hamlets to renovate was prohibitive and the dwellings were demolished in 1976.

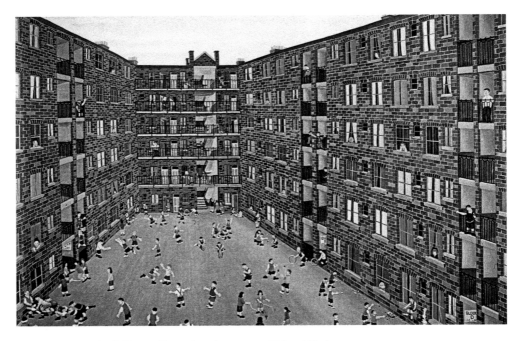

Charlotte de Rothschild Dwellings. (© The estate of John Allin)

In 1951, the 4 Per Cent changed its name to the Industrial Dwellings Society (IDS) and continues to manage a portfolio of social housing, including the surviving 4 Per Cent blocks.

# 9. The Man Who Became a Room

Dating from 1719, No. 19. Princelet Street is one of the oldest in the street and one that in no way prepares visitors for one of the most atmospheric interiors in Whitechapel, nor the stories the graceful unadorned frontage holds within.

The street was built as Princes Street and, together with Wilkes and Fournier streets, is one of three survivors of early eighteenth-century residential architecture to the west of Brick Lane.

As the Huguenots moved on, by the late nineteenth century the houses in these streets had become homes and workshops for Jewish migrants from Russia and Poland, who worked mostly in the garment trade, and the back yards were filled with outbuildings for storage and additional workrooms. By the 1970s, almost all of the Jewish businesses had closed and the streets experienced new immigrants, artists and designers who renovated the premises and created studios from former storage spaces. When Spitalfields Market relocated in 1991, regentrification began in earnest, with the houses now some of the most desirable in London.

However, No. 19 was to have a different destiny. An early family here were the Ogiers, French Huguenots whose daughter married into the Courtauld family. Their business,

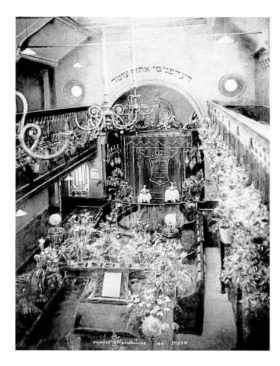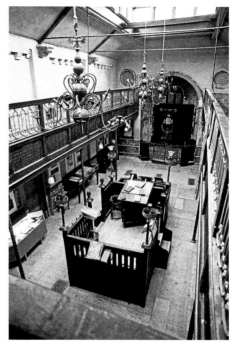

*Above left*: Princelet Street Synagogue decorated for the festival of Shavuot, *c.* 1911. (Courtesy of Ivan Reback)

*Above right*: The interior of Princelet Street Synagogue. (© The Jewish Museum, London)

founded in 1794, eventually became a world leader in textiles, chemicals and man-made fibres. After they, and subsequent residents, moved on, the house was acquired in 1869 by a small Polish community called the Loyal United Friends Friendly Society and they built a synagogue over the back garden.

The ladies' gallery was supported by slender pillars and above the reader's desk was a fan light of tinted green, yellow and pink glass providing as much light as possible in the days before electricity.

When the Federation of Minor Synagogues was established in 1887, Princes Street Synagogue, as it was then, was a founder member. At the height of the Jewish East End when the population numbered around 125,000 there were perhaps sixty-five synagogues. Most of them were 'steibels' (small orthodox communities) often numbering less than 100 members, and the majority belonged to the Federation.

Painted donation boards around the base of the ladies' gallery list support from both the wealthy (visitors will spot names such as Rothschild and Mocatta) and the poor who gave what they could. The poverty within the community meant the synagogue was a 'Penny Wedding' venue, where the marriage licence was subsidised by wealthy benefactors.

Despite the poverty, the synagogue was decorated for the Jewish festivals, as illustrated by a *c.* 1911 image when the interior was filled with floral decorations for Shavuoth

(Pentecost). Eventually, with the demise of the Jewish community, the federation closed the synagogue in 1963.

The building remained with a caretaker in attendance and the attic was rented to David Rodinsky, a scholar with a wide range of interests including Kabbalah (Jewish mysticism), London maps, gramophone records and Sanskrit. The synagogue gradually became forgotten until 1980, when the Spitalfields Historic Housing Trust acquired No. 17 and No. 19. On entering No. 19, they found the synagogue and historic interior features intact. Despite a covering of dust and cobwebs, the pews, reading desk, prayer books and prayer shawls were immediately discernible, providing an amazing insight to the look and feel of these East End 'schtiebels'. The peeling paint and crumbling brickwork only added to the atmosphere but also represented nearly two decades of neglect.

When the Trust went upstairs, an even more amazing sight met them. It was a room with a bed and rudimentary furniture but one filled with books, maps, scrapbooks, records and more. There were no photographs of anyone and it seemed the resident had left in haste. Writers and photographers visited and Iain Sinclair's article 'The Man who Became a Room' brought the story to the public's notice. Interest then waned until 1991, when a young woman researching her family history arrived at the synagogue where her grandparents had married. She found out that David Rodinsky had died in 1969 shortly before her birth, and with that link in place, she started researching his fate further. Having no family and falling ill, he was taken to the London Hospital (*see* entry No. 24), but unable to look after himself, he was moved to an asylum and his home closed up and forgotten.

The building is now administered by a charity, the Spitalfields Centre. With minimal renovations over the years the interior of this synagogue retains an atmospheric, eerie presence. Also known as the Museum of Immigration and Diversity, the synagogue is not generally open to the public, although it (but not David's room) can be viewed by appointment or on specified open days.

# 10. Looking Up

Christ Church Primary School on Brick Lane is one of the more picturesque buildings on the street. Founded as a charity school in 1708, the current building was completed in 1874 as a Church of England school linked to nearby Christ Church, Spitalfields.

The significant change in the area at the time was the influx of Jewish immigrants from Eastern Europe. Brick Lane was at the centre of what became the largest Jewish community in the UK by the beginning of the twentieth century, here in Whitechapel. Between 1880, when compulsory education was extended to 10 year olds, and the 1950s, it is likely that a significant proportion of children attending the primary school would have been Jewish.

Looking up to the right-hand side of the building, just below the roof, an unusual Victorian cast-iron water collector can be seen. It bears the symbol of the Jewish faith, the six-pointed star called a Magen David, or 'Star of David'.

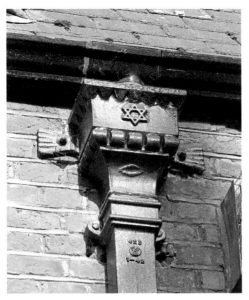

Christ Church School Water Collector.            Christ Church School Roundel.

There is no recorded evidence of why this exists. One belief is that the staff of the school wanted to make their Jewish charges feel at home and therefore decorated the building with this water collector. The other view is that decoration of water collectors was commonplace in Victorian times and it is by chance and not intention that it bears this symbol.

One feature that suggests that the design is more than chance are the unusually shaped flanges on either side of the main body that hold it to the wall. These five-ribbed side features may represent the 'Hamsa', an amulet found throughout the Middle East and North Africa. This symbol is believed by Jews and Muslims to provide protection against 'the evil eye'.

Whether it was accident or intention that led to this fixture being on a Church of England primary school, it remains a secret on Brick Lane that few discover, except by serendipity.

The star is seen by looking up. Looking down brings another discovery, a roundel decorated with children, a book and crayons (*see* entry No. 11).

# 11. History at Your Feet

When exploring a city, visitors are always encouraged to look up towards rooftops and gables and espy dates and names of often long-gone shops and pubs. In and around Brick Lane visitors are also encouraged to look down. There, at their feet, they will find works of art designed as manhole covers providing a delightful introduction to the area's history and heritage.

# SPITALFIELDS ROUNDELS BY KEITH BOWLER

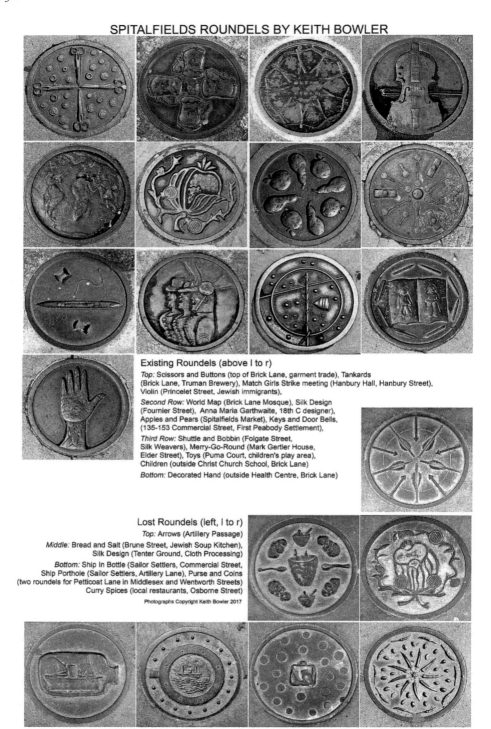

### Existing Roundels (above l to r)

*Top:* Scissors and Buttons (top of Brick Lane, garment trade), Tankards (Brick Lane, Truman Brewery), Match Girls Strike meeting (Hanbury Hall, Hanbury Street), Violin (Princelet Street, Jewish immigrants),

*Second Row:* World Map (Brick Lane Mosque), Silk Design (Fournier Street), Anna Maria Garthwaite, 18th C designer), Apples and Pears (Spitalfields Market), Keys and Door Bells, (135-153 Commercial Street, First Peabody Settlement),

*Third Row:* Shuttle and Bobbin (Folgate Street, Silk Weavers), Merry-Go-Round (Mark Gertler House, Elder Street), Toys (Puma Court, children's play area), Children (outside Christ Church School, Brick Lane)

*Bottom:* Decorated Hand (outside Health Centre, Brick Lane)

### Lost Roundels (left, l to r)

*Top:* Arrows (Artillery Passage)

*Middle:* Bread and Salt (Brune Street, Jewish Soup Kitchen), Silk Design (Tenter Ground, Cloth Processing)

*Bottom:* Ship In Bottle (Sailor Settlers, Commercial Street, Ship Porthole (Sailor Settlers, Artillery Lane), Purse and Coins (two roundels for Petticoat Lane in Middlesex and Wentworth Streets) Curry Spices (local restaurants, Osborne Street)

Photographs Copyright Keith Bowler 2017

Roundels.

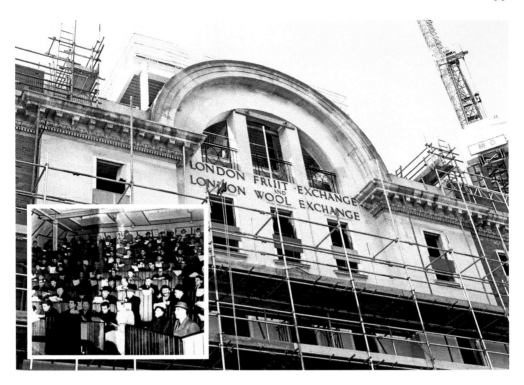

The London Fruit and Wool Exchange façade has been incorporated into a new development.

*Inset*: David Kira (seated in the centre of the fifth row, with glasses) in the auction room of the London Fruit and Wool Exchange.

They were commissioned in 1995 by the London Borough of Tower Hamlets from local artist Keith Bowler, but of the original twenty just thirteen remain.

Some are very straightforward with the link to the site self-explanatory. *Apples and Pears* outside Old Spitalfields Market on the corner of Brushfield Street and Commercial Street is a reminder of the wholesale fruit and vegetable market here between 1638 and 1991, when it relocated to Leyton. This roundel also links to the London Fruit and Wool Exchange on Brushfield Street. Built in 1929 as an auction house, the Fruit Exchange, wool trading arrived in 1963. Demolished in 2016, the site is nearing completion as a new office and retail complex. Incorporating a section of the original frontage, this is an example of 'façadism' (*see* entry No. 3).

On Brick Lane, *Scissors and Buttons* indicate the tailoring trade of the late nineteenth and twentieth centuries and *Bobbins* links to the earlier silk trade dominated by the French Huguenots. A *Globe*, also on Brick Lane, represents the different nations from which so many communities of Whitechapel have come. A favourite is the *Children, Books and Crayons* found outside Christ Church School (*see* entry No. 10), also on Brick Lane.

Some stories are not so obvious. The *Matchstick People* outside Hanbury Hall link to the 1888 Bryant & May Matchgirls' Strike in Bow. The Hall was used for meetings, gathering support and collecting much-needed funds for the strikers who were demanding better pay and an end to the use of dangerous yellow phosphorus.

The *Viola* on Princelet Street outside a late-1920s factory building, now apartments, commemorates the first purpose-built Yiddish theatre in London. A professional Yiddish theatre actor from Russia, Jacob Adler, raised funds and the Russian Hebrew Dramatic Club was built in 1886. In 1887, someone shouted 'Fire!' during a sell-out performance and in the audience's haste to escape seventeen people died in the crush. There had been no fire and the theatre, unable to survive this tragedy, closed not long after. Jacob left for America but returned regularly to London where Yiddish Theatre remained in the East End until the closure of the Grand Palais on Commercial Road, in 1970.

Outside No. 32 Elder Street, where a Blue Plaque commemorates the home of East End artist Mark Gertler, the roundel depicts three people in side-relief. They are an interpretation of a detail from Gertler's most famous work, the brightly coloured 'Merry-Go-Round', painted in 1916 as an anti-war polemic. Funded by the Jewish Educational Aid Society to attend Slade School of Art, Gertler subsequently entered the literary and artistic world of the Bloomsbury Set. He committed suicide in 1939 at his Hampstead studio, with the rolled-up canvas of the unsold 'Merry-Go-Round' beside him. Now owned by Tate Britain, the painting is on public display.

To the younger generation the roundel in Puma Court, a traffic-free zone linking Commercial Street to Wilkes Street, looks like a depiction of the solar system. Round dots of differing sizes are displayed randomly alongside what looks like a beehive and candy sticks. However, this roundel is a reminder of a play area for local children where they could play safely with their spinning tops and marbles.

Roundels that have gone missing represented other important stories of the area including the *Arrows* of the artillery ground, later developed as the network of streets centred on Artillery Lane and Passage (*see* entry No. 3) and Gun Street, the *Salt and Bread* linked to the Jewish Soup Kitchen, whose ornate frontage remains on Brune Street, and the *Spices* represented the Bengali curry houses which, until recently, dominated Brick Lane but which are now being replaced by sushi, pizza and organic chocolate.

## 12. Bohemian Rhapsody on Osborn Street

Osborn Street is a small stubby offshoot of Brick Lane connecting with Whitechapel High Street at the southern end.

Half way along is Osborn House, a white painted, two-storey, post-war office building. Prominently displayed are signs for a solicitor and an accountant but by the entrance a discrete sign indicates London Recording Studio.

This is just the latest incarnation of a recording studio on the premises with a heritage which places it in the highest level of 'Rock Royalty'. Originally the City of London Recording Studios, it was bought in 1973 by brother and sister Jill and John Sinclair, and when a successful musician turned producer, Trevor Horn, joined them it was incorporated into his SARM Studios (later SARM East, to distinguish from a second studio on the other side of London in Notting Hill Gate).

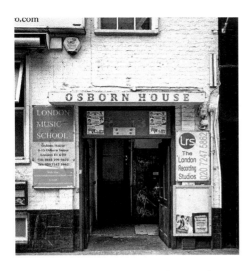
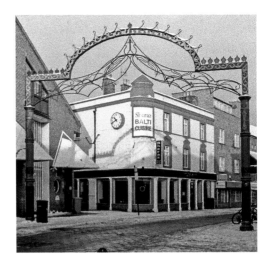

*Above left*: The London Recording Studios in Osborn Street.

*Above right*: Banglatown Arch, entrance to Brick Lane.

The list of musicians and bands who recorded at SARM East reads like a veritable constellation of some of the biggest names in music of their time. Parts of 'Bohemian Rhapsody' by Queen were recorded here in 1975 and other artists that used the studios include Madonna, The Clash, Yes, ABC, Seal, INXS and Frankie Goes to Hollywood.

Hopefully, in thirty years' time, another writer will make an equally stellar list of acts from those artists recording there now. Standing in front of the studios, to your right in the distance is Meena Thakor's arch, erected in 1997 and signalling the start of Brick Lane and the entrance to Banglatown.

# 13. Changes at Itchy Park

Across the road from Aldgate East tube, an Islamic-style metal arch erected in 1989 entices visitors into Altab Ali Park but before they enter their gaze is taken by something much older. The Victorian drinking fountain alongside was erected in 1860 on the Whitechapel Road. It was an early example of fountains providing Londoners with filtered water through the Metropolitan Drinking Fountain Association, founded a year earlier by Quaker banker Samuel Gurney. The initiative was an immediate success with cattle troughs being added from 1867. Once ubiquitous across the Capital, only a few remain and mostly relocated from their original road-side positions. Often funded in memory of a family member or distinguished person, this fountain is described as 'from one unknown yet well known'.

Through the arch, this small enclave of green has been a public space since 1966. Originally St Mary's Park, it was renamed in 1994 to commemorate a young Asian tailor, Altab Ali, murdered in Adler Street alongside the park on his way home from work in May 1978. The 1970s was an uncomfortable period in the history of the East End. The growing Bengali community faced racism, discrimination and violence on a daily basis.

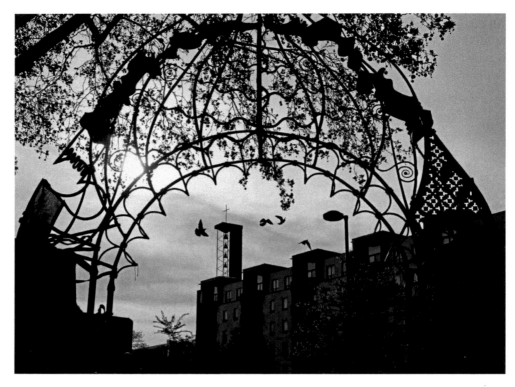

Altab Ali Park.

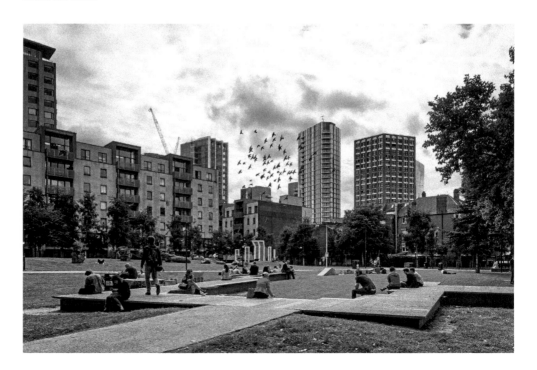

Ali's death became a rallying cry to bring their experiences to the public's notice. On the day of Ali's funeral, a procession of 7,000 people walked with his coffin through central London, reaching Downing Street to demand action from the government. In 2016, the London Borough of Tower Hamlets designated each 4 May as an annual Altab Ali Commemoration Day

In 1999, a smaller version of the Shaheed Minar or Martyrs' Memorial in Dhaka, Bangledesh was unveiled in the park. Different sized white metal fence-like structures with a big red circle behind represent a mother, four children and spilled blood. This and the original in Dhaka commemorate those killed in the student riots in February 1952 when Urdu was proclaimed the official language of East Pakistan over the more widely spoken Bengali. Subsequently, the two languages were given dual status and the United Nations designated 21 February each year as Mother Tongue Day.

Recent re-landscaping in 2011 incorporated undulating grassy hillocks, boulders and a low stone wall outlining the footprint of the church of St Mary Matfelon before its almost total destruction in 1940 during the Blitz and demolition in 1952.

In centuries past, those living near Aldgate had a long walk to worship at their parish church, St Dunstan's in Stepney, so they were designated a chapel of ease. Built of stone rubble on this site, it was rebuilt in the 1400s and painted white. It became known as the White Chapel, giving this area of east London its name and was later rebuilt in the late nineteenth century.

The burial ground was closed in the 1850s. Most graves were cleared during the subsequent rebuilding but a couple of impressive sarcophagus tombs remain. Famous burials (although the exact sites are not known) were Richard Brandon, a royal executioner and credited with the dubious honour of beheading King Charles I in 1649, and Sir John Cass, a local merchant, City MP and philanthropist whose legacy now funds four education establishments in his name.

Today this small public place, once one of London's 'Itchy Parks' where the homeless would spend their days before finding refuge at night in local shelters, is used more than ever before but now as a haven for weekend visitors and office workers at lunchtime.

## DID YOU KNOW?

Altab Ali Park is overshadowed on one side by the new high-rise steel and glass of Goodman Fields apartment blocks and on the other by the modern bell-tower of St Boniface that dominates. Originally established in 1875 for Whitechapel's German Roman Catholic community, it was destroyed during the Second World War and rebuilt in 1959. It incorporates several 1912 Stations of the Cross which survived with new bells for the campanile made at the nearby Whitechapel Bell Foundry.

# 14. Anarchist Faces

Alongside the Whitechapel Art Gallery a narrow passage, Angel Alley, leads to the Freedom Bookshop, an independent publisher and outlet specialising in books on radicals, anarchists, revolutionaries and all forms of social activism. Founded in 1886, it is the longest surviving anarchist press in the English-speaking world and has been at this site since 1968.

On the left-hand wall is a large black and white mural depicting thirty-six faces in silhouette. At first glance, there is something that seems out of kilter. It takes a moment to realise the names are ordered alphabetically by first name rather than a traditional listing by surname. Known as the Anarchist Mural, it celebrates those who railed against conformity and the establishment whether here or abroad. Designed in collaboration with the Freedom Press, it is based on a series of cards they published in 1994, designed in a woodcut style by artist Clifford Harper, a committed anarchist who once lived locally in a Stepney Green squat.

East London is the spiritual home of effecting social change, witnessing the birth of key movements in the struggle for worker's rights, free speech and gender equality. It was Whitechapel that proved a haven for European anarchists and revolutionaries hounded out from the mainland (*see* entry No. 21) and in October 1936 it was in Whitechapel where Jewish, communist and dock communities prevented a Fascist march culminating in the famous Battle of Cable Street.

The mural illustrates the international scale of London's activists with figures from around the world including Germany, Russia, France and America. German Rudolph

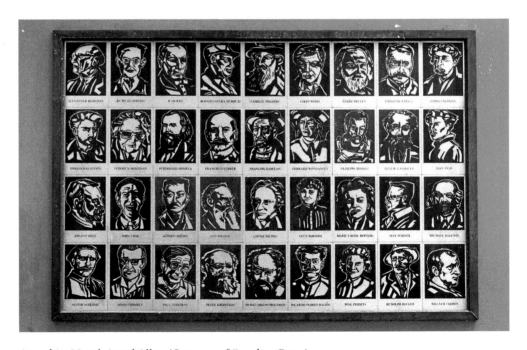

Anarchist Mural, Angel Alley. (Courtesy of Freedom Press)

Rocker (*see* entry No. 35) is resplendent with a large brimmed hat. Italian-born Erico Malatesta spent most of his life in exile. Having met Peter Kropotkin in Switzerland, he subsequently lived on and off in London for nearly forty years as a regular visitor at Dunstan Houses. He ran a workshop in Islington where George Gardenstein, a felon linked

## DID YOU KNOW?

Near Angel Alley, on the doorway at No. 88 Whitechapel High Street is a large metal badge with an ornate Star of David supported on each side by Lions of Judah with a menorah (seven-branched candlestick) below. Designed by Arthur Szyk, it was the emblem of the *Jewish Daily Post* for their new premises in 1934–35. Established in 1926 as an English language Jewish newspaper, it ceased publication in 1935 shortly after the refurbishment.

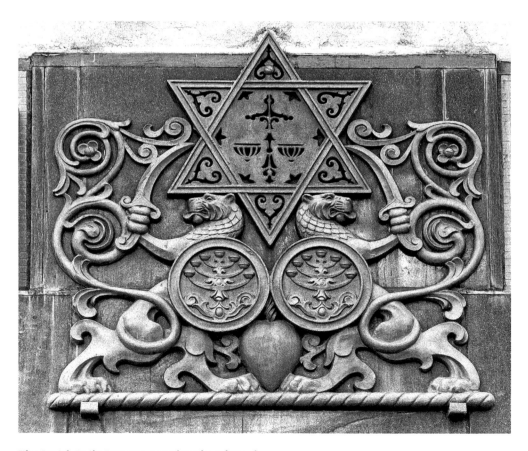

The *Jewish Daily Post* sign on Whitechapel Road.

to the Houndsditch burglary and the Siege of Sidney Street (*see* entry No. 31), obtained equipment for his crime.

Peter, actually Prince Peter, born in Russia, was the titular leader of the East End anarchists, founding the Freedom Press shortly after his arrival in London in 1886. He and his supporters were already publishing the journal *Freedom,* which only ceased publication in 2014 when the anarchist community migrated to online content.

William Godwin was the husband of Mary Wollstonecraft, known as the 'Mother of Feminism' and a notable absence from the mural; she died in 1797 shortly after giving birth to their daughter, Mary, who later married Percy Bysshe Shelley and wrote the novel *Frankenstein.*

Among the women who are represented is Louise Michel who, in the early 1890s, established the International Anarchist School in Fitzrovia. A French anarchist, she had fought on the barricades during the Paris Commune and after several periods of imprisonment went into exile, living in Russia and Germany before moving to London in 1890.

# 15. Street Signs

We take for granted today that wherever we are in London we can identify our location using clearly displayed street names. Increasingly, navigation systems on smart phones indicate location and the routes to any destination.

However, London streets did not always have signs stating their names. The turning point in street signage came after the Great Fire of London in 1666. There was a realisation that any kind of public assistance system would only work if you could identify streets clearly. Even before a series of laws passed in the early eighteenth century requiring all streets in London to have name boards pinned to a wall, some streets were already identified by plaster tablets bearing the street name and year of the sign.

Whitechapel is lucky to bear three fine examples but you must go hunting for them. The oldest tablet street sign is right on the southern border of Whitechapel and adorns the entrance to a now closed public house, The Rose, at No. 128 The Highway. It bears the legend 'This is the corner of Chigwell Streate' and is dated 1678, relatively soon after the Great Fire. It is a mystery as to how the tablet became embedded in the wall of a Victorian public house. This sign may well be one of the oldest surviving tablet street signs in London.

The second oldest sign is at the northern end of Whitechapel, at the corner of Brick Lane and Sclater Street. It bears the date 1708. It is also of an ornate design, possibly indicating that at the time Sclater Street had some importance or standing in the area. It is remembered chiefly for the bird market, with the chirping of linnets, nightingales and canaries lasting well into the twentieth century. Below, are seen contemporary street signs in both English and Bengali, reflecting the new demographic of the area.

The third sign is tucked away on the wall of the former Whitechapel Bell Foundry building on Plumbers Row, and states, 'This is Baynes Street 1746'. It too has obviously been transplanted and relates back to a former name for the street.

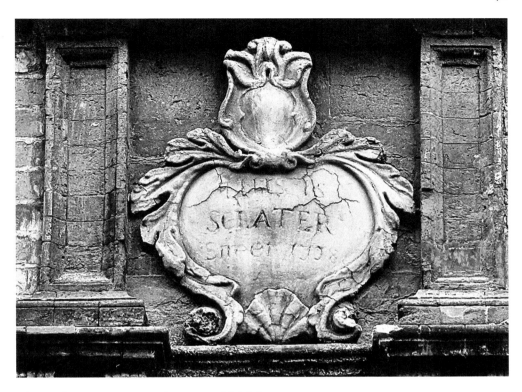

*Above*: Sclater Street sign on the corner of Brick Lane.

*Below left*: Chigwell Street sign on the corner of The Highway.

*Below right*: Baynes Street (now Plumbers Row).

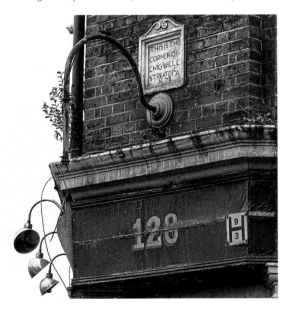

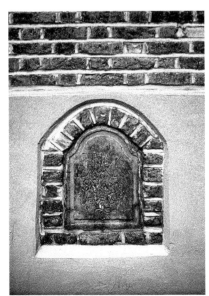

The aesthetics of these three signs vary from utilitarian to intricate – a possible indication of the social aspiration of the streets – and they also span the period from the end of the Stuarts to the reign of the Hanoverian monarchs, and the growth of modern London through trade and immigration.

## 16. Underneath the Arches

Pedley Street stretches along the northern edge of Whitechapel from Vallance Road to Brick Lane. At one time a straight run, it is now two sections divided by the graceful sweeping embankment of the Overground line.

The eastern end still carries trains into nearby Liverpool Street Station and alongside is an abandoned railway viaduct which carried freight into the vast Bishopsgate goods yard until it closed in 1964 following a fire. Since then it has remained derelict but at the time of writing awaits redevelopment.

Just beyond Weaver House on Pedley Street a sharp turn creates the dead end, Fleet Street Hill, which runs under a railway arch, the last remaining section of the viaduct.

Known as the Pedley Street Arch, it is clearly seen from Brick Lane and even more so since its refurbishment as part of the new Overground railway opened in 2010, when it became a magnet for graffiti, now more affectionately known as street art.

Connected by a footbridge to Cheshire Street, it has long had a sinister and disreputable association. It was the ideal spot for the homeless, the inebriated and even the lovelorn to

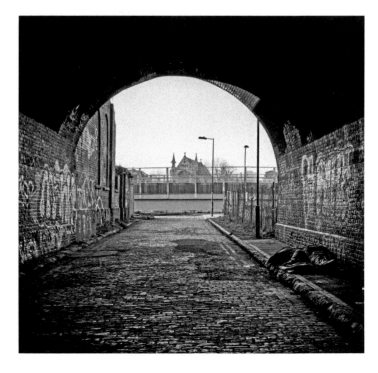

Dossing in the Pedley Street Arch in 2014.

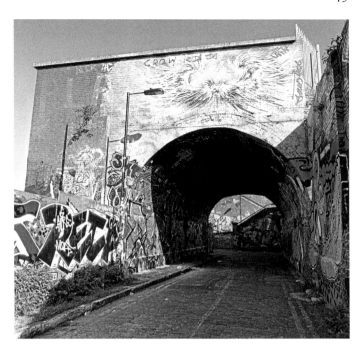

Pedley Street Arch in 2017.

take shelter in the semi or complete darkness, depending on the time of day. Descriptions are of a foul smelling, dark and foreboding shortcut to the other side of the tracks.

Author Emanuel Litvinoff, who grew up in Whitechapel, preserved the arch in literature in his semi-autobiographical *Journey Through a Small Planet*. One night his mother appoints him as the guardian of a young female friend of the family and he accompanies her back to her home in Whitechapel taking a route through the arch. He observed:

> There were no unusual signs of debauchery when we came to the railway arch although couples grappled against the dripping walls and tramps lay around parcelled in old newspaper. The evil of the place was in its gloom, its putrid stench, in the industrial grime of half a century with which it was impregnated. The sinister possibilities excited me: I was not immune to the *dybbuk,* after all.

'Dybbuk' is Yiddish for a malicious spirit that possesses the body.

As film-makers and photographers look for a touch of the authentic down-at-heel, albeit rapidly disappearing, East End, it is not unsurprising that the arch found new fame. Today, you are just as likely to find a model or musician doing a photo-shoot as you are to find people encased in sleeping bags using it as a shelter for a night's 'kip'.

Guy Ritchie's East-End fable *Lock, Stock and Two Smoking Barrels* (1998) used it as a location and it appeared briefly as a scene in Alfonso Cuarón's dystopian view of the future, *Children of Men* (2006). On television, amongst other appearances, the arch was a location in the third series of *Luther*, featuring a grim scene when Luther's police partner DS Ripley was gunned down.

# 17. The Spitalfields Gourd

Dotted around London are sixteen City Farms including one in Buxton Street, Spitalfields. These urban oases provide local residents with the chance to experience farmyard animals and freshly grown local produce. The first City Farm was opened in 1972 in Kentish Town, north London, and there are now over 120 throughout the UK. In London, they are sited mostly to the east and north and the London Borough of Tower Hamlets has three: Mudchute, Spitalfields and Stepney, opened in 1974, 1978 and 1979, respectively.

Spitalfields City Farm lies between Buxton Street and the Overground railway, in sight of Brick Lane and in the shadow of the Truman Brewery complex. Previously wasteland, it was converted into allotments for those who had lost their land to developers. Visitors are welcomed to the complex by a giant stone *Ram and Magpie*, created by sculptor Paula Haughney, based in Bromley-by-Bow, east London.

There is a country feel to the farm, with cobbled pathways and wooden fences delineating the various areas for animals, plants and grassland for grazing. The livestock, including pigs, sheep, ponies, goats and chickens, provides an oasis of rural life for local children, with the trains alongside bringing everyone back to reality.

A testimony to the popularity and affection for the farm is the crowd at the annual Goat Race, which takes place on the same day as London's Boat Race. The yurt, used for community events and activities, is also available for hire, the farm needing to maintain regular income to survive (its site is prime real estate and under regular threat from property developers).

As you enter the farm, a sign made out of bottle tops ushers you towards the Coriander Club Garden, a gardening and cookery club established for local Bengali women 1999 by Lutfun Hussain. Born in East Pakistan (now Bangladesh) Lutfun arrived in London in 1969 with her husband, and unable to find familiar vegetables, grew her own.

Using knowledge she had acquired from her own gardening, she began volunteering at the farm in 1999 and named her club after her nation's favourite herb. She later became an Ethnic Minority Support Worker and then a Healthy Living Co-Ordinator. Inspiring local women to grow vegetables and herbs for their home cooking, at the same time the club provided an opportunity for socialising. Many of the women had not yet learnt English or were tied to the domestic world of their home, rarely venturing outside. Growing vegetables linked to their homeland also alleviated a sense of yearning for what they had left behind.

Lutfun has become something of a celebrity, having been chosen as a member of the Sustainable Development Commission, publishing a recipe book, and proving an inspirational speaker at events promoting organic horticulture and healthy eating. The produce has also attained celebrity status. She has managed to cultivate the blackish-purple flat lablab beans, native to Africa, loofahs and yard-long beans, but her biggest challenge was to grow kodu, a large bottle-shaped gourd. Several hang proudly inside the polytunnels and when they grew to full size they were featured in the national press.

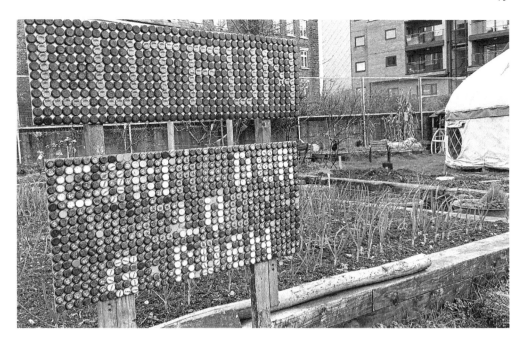

Lutfun Coriander Club sign. (© Rachel Kolsky)

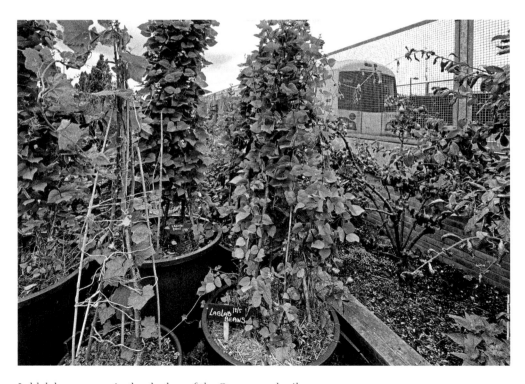

Lablab beans grow in the shadow of the Overground railway.

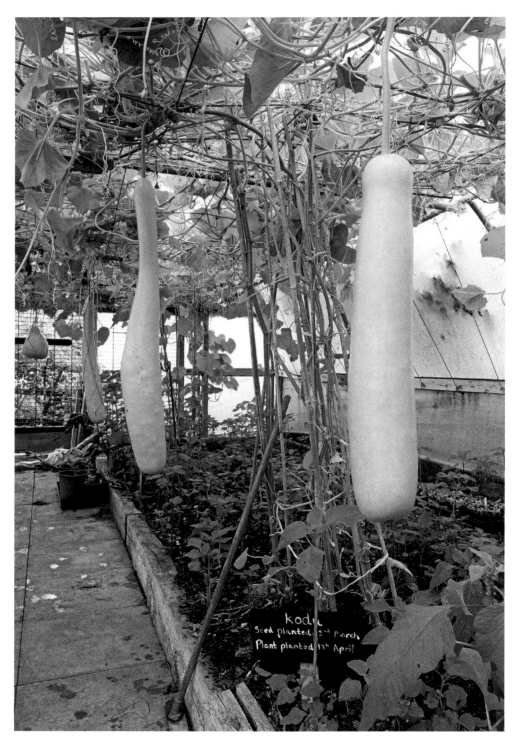

Kodu gourds ripening at the Coriander Club.

# 18. Mother Levy's

In Underwood Road, newly built blocks of social housing by the Peabody Trust and the London Borough of Tower Hamlets have been named Bearsted and Ada Lewis Courts. At first glance, these angular designed homes look plain and unadorned. However, the exterior incorporates stone lettering recounting a story of Jewish philanthropy and social work linked to the health of mothers and babies of the early twentieth-century local Jewish community.

The first Lord Bearsted, Marcus Samuel, who founded Shell Transport and Trading in 1897, and Ada Lewis, the widow of moneylender and philanthropist Samuel Lewis, both supported the initiative of Alice Model to provide facilities for the increasing number of Jewish births in Whitechapel. Alice had already successfully launched two initiatives. The Sick Rooms Help Society, founded in 1895, funded home-helps to assist the sick poor in their own homes. The Jewish Day Nursery (now the Alice Model Nursery in Stepney), established in 1897 in Spitalfields, provided day care for children of working mothers. Alice then turned her attention to maternity care.

With financial backing from wealthy supporters and those who donated in kind such as Harris Lebus, the furniture company, the Jewish Maternity Hospital opened in 1911 in two gabled cottage-style houses. A second building opened in 1925 as the Childrens' Welfare

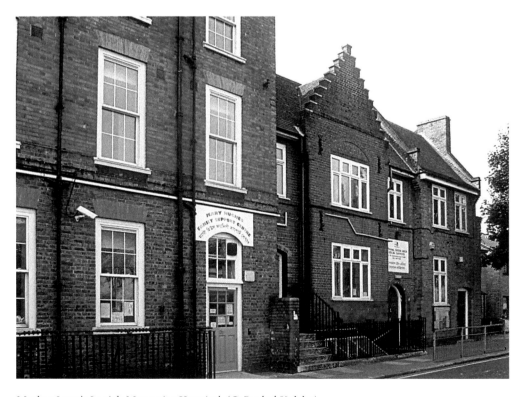

Mother Levy's Jewish Maternity Hospital. (© Rachel Kolsky)

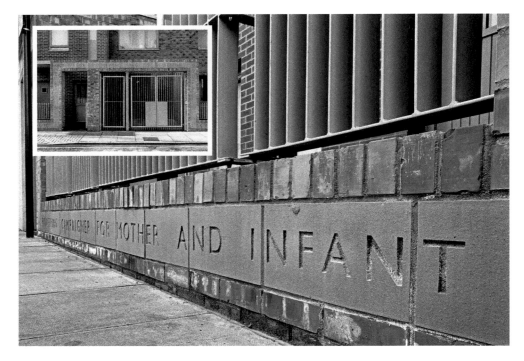

Ada Lewis and Bearsted Courts, decorated with the history of Mother Levy's.

Centre and, as demand for beds increased, a third phase was completed in 1927, providing four new wards, a nursery and accommodation for midwives and administrators. Alice ran the hospital from 1911 until her death in 1943, with the name changing to the Bearsted Memorial Hospital in 1940.

By the mid-1930s, around 800 babies were being born there each year, but with an increasing number of Jewish people migrating to the suburbs plans were made to relocate to Stoke Newington. With the outbreak of the Second World War, the hospital was evacuated to Hampton Court, and in 1947 it reopened in purpose-built premises on Lordship Road. It closed in 1974.

In 1947, following the maternity home relocating, the Whitechapel site was renamed the Mary Hughes Family Centre after the social worker and JP who lived close by and whose name was already well known through Hughes Mansions on Vallance Road. Despite a vociferous campaign to have the buildings listed to prevent the recent redevelopment, the hospital was demolished in 2012.

With nothing of the original structures remaining, it is the stone lettering which unlocks its secrets, including the name Sarah Levy, the District Maternity Superintendent of the Sick Rooms Help Society which had been linked with the maternity hospital since the latter's inception. No one was ever told they were born at the Jewish Maternity Hospital, it was known to everyone as Mother Levy's.

# 19. Light Is My Glory

Whitechapel still bears evidence of the Education Acts of the latter part of the nineteenth century in the form of the many School Board of London (SBL) premises built in the last two decades of the century.

In February 1896, the Deal Street Elementary School opened on the corner of Hanbury Street. It was designed to provide places for up to 1,250 children (which hints at the size of the population in the area at the time) and is representative in terms of design and style of many similar schools of the era.

These schools have impressive and imposing exteriors. This building is solid brick with vermillion-coloured horizontal bands and vertical columns to outline windows, corners and edges. Some windows are dressed in Portland stone masonry. In keeping with several other schools in the area (which often had little or no space at street level), the playground was on the roof and secured by tall railings.

As with other Board schools, there is a prominent plaque with the name of the school and the date it was opened (although in this case it is dated the year before it opened). In the gable end, there is a large bas-relief, unnoticed to the casual passer-by.

It depicts a pair of children, a boy and a girl, being tutored by a man and woman, presumably their teachers. At the top of the frieze is the SBL motto, '*Lux Mihi Laus*' or Light is My Glory. Then as now, it was believed that education was the 'light' through which the life chances of young people would be improved.

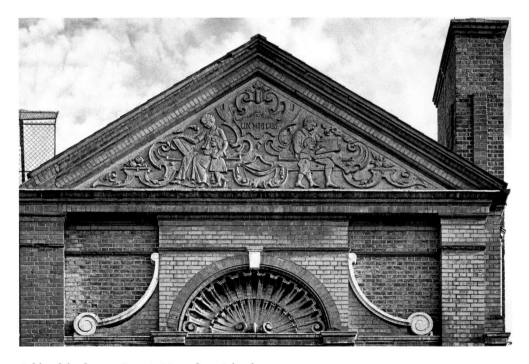

Gable of the former Captain Montefiore School.

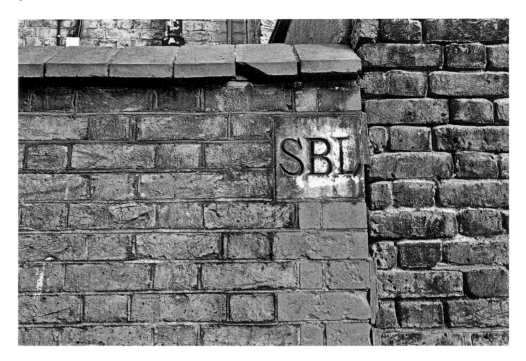

The School Board of London initials etched into a brick on the school wall.

The quality of the construction, the ornamentation and the additional expense of items like the bas-relief all point to an organisation aiming to impress the populace with its power and the importance of the services it provided.

At some later point, possibly 1915 or 1916, the name of the school changed to the Captain Robert Sebag-Montefiore Elementary and Secondary School. Robert was related to one of the wealthiest Jewish philanthropists of the Victorian era, Sir Moses Montefiore. Before the First World War, Robert had trained as a barrister and became a member of the London County Council, where he was vice-chair of the Education Committee. Serving with the Royal East Kent Mounted Rifles, he was sent to the ill-fated Gallipoli peninsula, where he was wounded and later died, aged 34, in 1915 after being evacuated to Alexandria, Egypt. The school was renamed by the London County Council in recognition of his sacrifice and his contribution to education in London.

## 20. Hopetown

The small square park Vallance Gardens is named after its neighbouring road of the same name. Established in the seventeenth century as a Quaker burial ground, in the late nineteenth century it was leased to the council and laid out as a public garden. Today, Vallance Gardens still contains two original Victorian marble drinking fountains, although they no longer spout water.

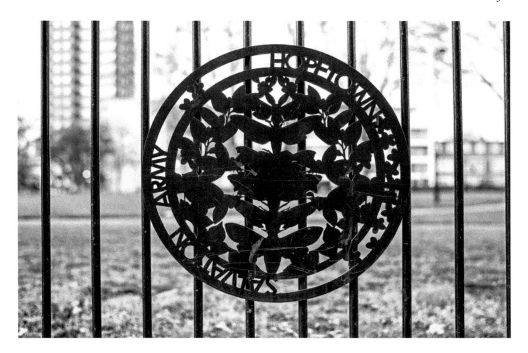

*Above*: Hopetown Roundel in Vallance Gardens.

*Below left*: Hopetown resident with drum. (© The Salvation Army International Heritage Centre)

*Below right*: Hopetown Street on the corner of Brick Lane.

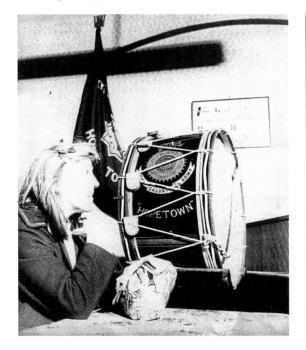

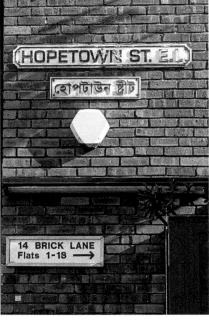

In the early twenty-first century, the park was re-landscaped and encircled by new railings. As part of the decoration, several roundels were embedded with titles and designs relating to the local area.

One roundel is that of Swanlea. Not to be confused with the village of the same name in Kent, the Whitechapel Swanlea was a small pond in the vicinity and now the name of a secondary school in nearby Brady Street.

Another roundel bears the title 'Hopetown' relating to the activities of William Booth and the Salvation Army in Whitechapel (*see* also entry No. 28). At one time, before the public gardens were laid out, he preached in a tent erected here.

William's mission was not just to preach his religion but also to help improve the conditions of the residents of the East End, whose lives were blighted by levels of terrible poverty which are almost unimaginable today. Like many nineteenth-century philanthropists, he was acutely aware of the level of homelessness amongst the population and in the 1880s the Salvation Army commenced creating night shelters, which offered a bed, food and, above all, safety.

Florence Booth, a daughter-in-law of William and Catherine, was instrumental in improving conditions that women endured in the East End. The first refuge opened at No. 212 Hanbury Street. It closed in 1885, moving to Dalston, but in 1889 the Army returned to Hanbury Street, opening a Women's Hostel known as the Hope Town shelter (up until the 1932 move the centre was known simply as 'The Hanbury Street Shelter') at No. 194/196 Hanbury Street. It catered for women only, with a special section for women with children. The shelters charged for their services but their facilities were cheaper than the commercial 'doss' houses. A survey conducted later in its life found that one woman using Hope Town had done so continuously for almost twenty years. The Hope Town shelter continued into the 1930s, although the location switched to a former school in Finch Street just off Brick Lane. Today, that street been renamed Hopetown Street.

In 2006, the Salvation Army opened a modern women-only hostel, now called Hopetown, in nearby Old Montague Street, perpetuating the name and the welfare services for women. In 2017 plans were announced to relocate residents to new premises on the Isle of Dogs with the men at Booth House on Whitechapel Road moving to Hopetown.

## 21. The Revolutionary Door in Fulbourne Street

Fulbourne Street is a peculiar little side street in the centre of Whitechapel with a surprising historical secret.

At the turn of the century, Whitechapel had a large population of Eastern European immigrants. The Jewish immigrants were fleeing intolerable persecution and pogroms encouraged by the Russian Tsarist regime. Along with this group, there were also many dissidents from a range of political persuasions, from socialists to anarchists who, if they remained in their countries, were likely to be arrested, imprisoned and tortured by the authorities.

Despite curbs placed on immigration by the Aliens Act of 1905, the right to political asylum remained and indeed there was a public fascination with revolutionaries who

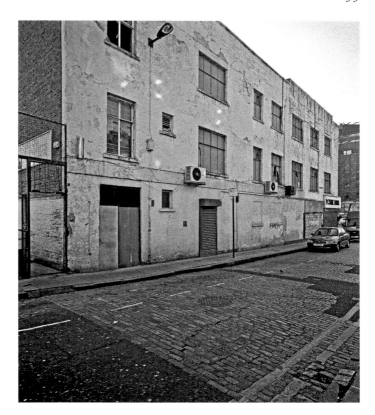

*Right*: The 'revolutionary' door.

*Below*: The current doorway.

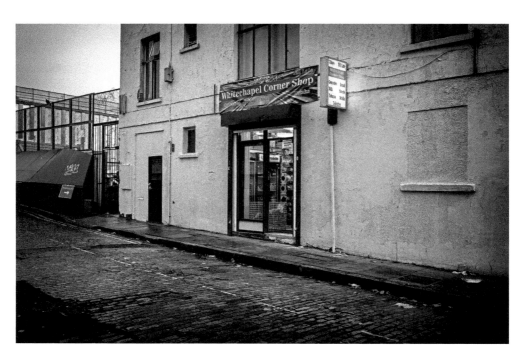

were seen to be aiming to achieve the kind of liberal democracy that Britain itself increasingly enjoyed since the Reform Acts of the nineteenth century.

In May 1907, 300 delegates arrived in London to attend the 5th Annual Congress of the Russian Social Democratic Labour Party. Although the main meeting itself took place at the Brotherhood Church, a Fabian institute in Hackney, a contingent of over 100 Bolsheviks held a separate meeting in an unremarkable building in Whitechapel, the Fulbourne Street headquarters of the Social Democratic Party.

The respected East End historian, Professor William Fishman, identified the green door in the photograph as the entrance through which, on one day in May 1907, walked Lenin, Stalin, Trotsky, Gorky and Litvinov, all to become fathers of the Bolshevik revolution of 1917.

Stalin and Litvinov remained in Whitechapel for some time after the main and separate congresses finished. During the two-week conference Stalin, then known as Joseph Djugashvili, and Litvinoff stayed at Tower House, made famous as the 'Monster Doss House' by writers Jack London and George Orwell.

Despite subsequently remaining in Whitechapel, living in Jubilee Street, it has been said that Stalin never spoke of his time in England. Some may see this door as unremarkable but the secret it holds is that some of the most important and notorious men and women of the twentieth century once graced this entrance and the building within, at a time when their future significance was unknown.

## 22. Plotting and Protesting

On Fieldgate Street, at the corner of Parfett Street, stands a small bedraggled building. At street level, an early piece of art by street artist Stik remains and colourful letters, 'L' 'A' 'R' and 'C', have been painted above the entrance. At first glance the lettering seems to belong to a children's nursery but on closer examination, flyers for events affixed to the windows testify that this is the London Action Resource Centre (LARC).

LARC is a social action collective established in 1999, originally known as 'The Fieldgate'. Self-organised and non-hierarchical, it needed a centre for meetings and this site was perfect, being situated at the heart of an area famous for radicals and revolutionaries. Nestling in the shadow of Tower House where, in 1907, both Stalin and Litvinov stayed for a few nights the Freedom Press (see entry No. 14) is also close by.

Ironically, but pragmatically, the group bought the premises and spent three years renovating it. Owning property also necessitated arranging legal footing as a limited company and fulfilling all the associated administrative criteria, such as insurance and health and safety.

Officially opened for business in 2002, it is foremost a resource centre where different groups can make banners, use the library, access the Internet and co-ordinate campaigns, including saving pubs, planning squats and protesting effectively.

Several of the most famous direct action groups have met here, including Reclaim the Streets and People's Global Action.

Looking up at the gabled roofline, the architecture suggests its original use. It was built in the 1860s as a Mission Hall and in 1921 became an International Modern School following the ethos of Louise Michel and Fernando Ferrer, both of whom are depicted on the Anarchist Mural (see entry No. 14).

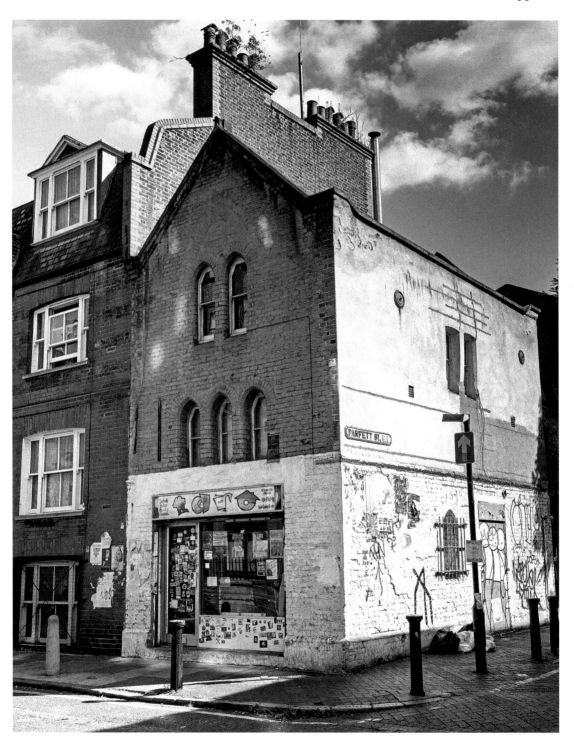

London Action Resource Centre.

Opening with thirty children, within a few months there were over 100, all being educated in 'the spirit of freedom'. Their classes included singing, storytelling and clay modelling. Older students were taught hygiene and social science. After closing in 1928, it became a synagogue and was later used by a succession of different tailoring and leather businesses. After a period of time lying empty and later used as storage for the garment trade, the building was vacated and left to decay before its new life began as this centre for social action.

# 23. Angels and Cherubs

Opposite the Royal London Hospital on Whitechapel Road is the Edward VII Memorial Drinking Fountain. Surmounted by a bronze angel and surrounded by market stalls, it stands mostly unnoticed by the locals passing by, hurrying for their morning coffees or concentrating on the giant frozen fish and colourful garments of Whitechapel Market.

But for those who have a moment to stop and look there is so much to enjoy. The fountain was erected in 1911 in 'grateful and loyal memory' and as a 'Thank You' to King Edward VII from the East End Jewish community. Many were recent migrants to London, arriving in the late nineteenth and early twentieth centuries during which time the Jewish population swelled to over 125,000. It slowed following the 1905 Aliens Act, which prevented further mass immigration but the Jewish community who had found refuge prior to the Act wanted to acknowledge the welcome they had been given by the king.

His likeness, adorned with the emblem of the Order of the Garter, is represented as a medallion on the southern side and an explanatory inscription is on the north side. On the sides of the obelisk stand a figure of Justice with scales in her left hand and a sword in her right and a winged figure of Liberty holding a scroll.

However, it is the cherubs at each corner which delight. One holds a ship representing the mode of transport the immigrants would have used, arriving in London not far from this spot near the Tower of London before reaching Whitechapel. Another cherub holds a book. Education was the key to escaping the East End and in addition to childrens' secular education at LSB (London School Board) schools or one of the two Jewish establishments, Jews' Free School and Stepney Jewish School, there were also Jewish studies after school and on Sundays at the various Talmud Torahs (literally Learning of the Law) and Cheders (literally Rooms in Yiddish). A third cherub sits sewing fabric with a needle and thread. For the East End Jewish community, the garment trade remained their predominant industry until the 1970s. A car held by the fourth cherub represents the shift from horse and carts to motor vehicles for those embracing the modernity of the early twentieth century.

King Edward looks towards the Royal London Hospital where his wife, Queen Alexandra, became President in 1904. Until recently, her statue was situated in a courtyard accessed via the grand front entrance and husband and wife could look towards each other, albeit with the building in between. Alexandra has now been relocated (*see* entry No. 25) and the original hospital buildings are due to be transformed into a new Town Hall for the London Borough of Tower Hamlets, providing Edward with a new and vibrant setting to look towards.

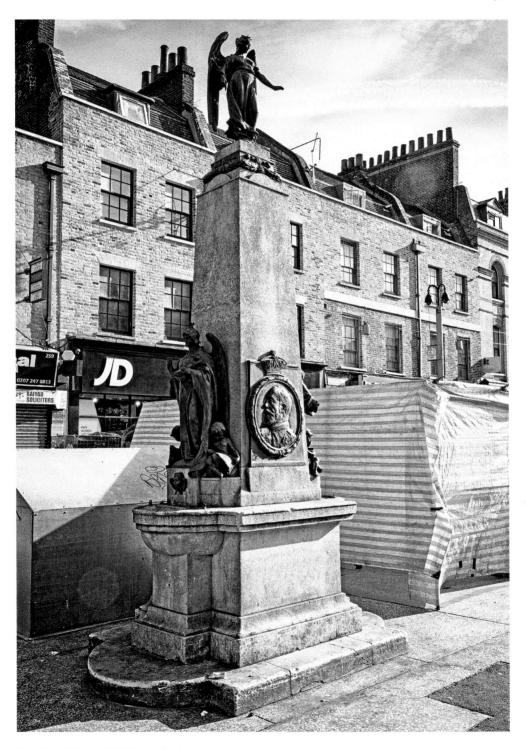

The King Edward VII Memorial Fountain.

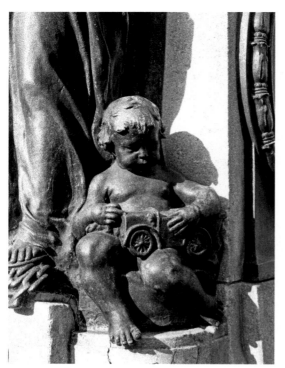
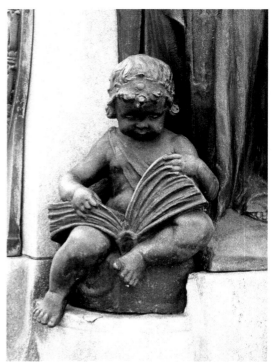
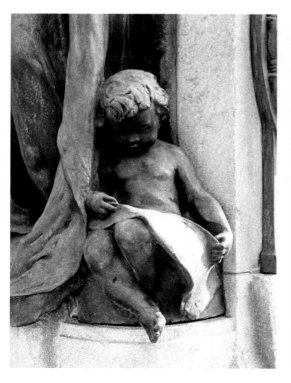
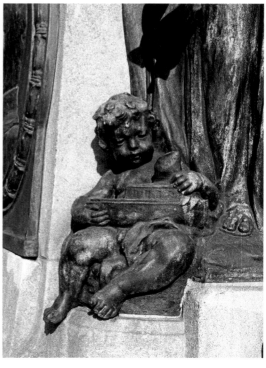

# 24. 'The London'

There is nothing secret about the impact of the Royal London Hospital on the landscape and the lives of Whitechapel. The original Georgian building with Victorian additions on Whitechapel Road is now overlooked by even more imposing modern state-of-the-art hospital buildings.

The Royal London Hospital (known locally as 'The London') began life in the 1740s in Moorgate but arrived in the countryside of Whitechapel in 1753. It expanded throughout the nineteenth and twentieth centuries before its transformation into an entirely new building in 2012. The original buildings will continue their valuable contribution to the area, being transformed into a new town hall for the London Borough of Tower Hamlets, its home borough.

Before the invention of electric light, natural light was invaluable for operating theatres. It was common in early hospitals for these to be placed at the top of buildings, allowing as much sunlight as possible to enter the rooms.

There are many important people associated with 'The London' who sadly over time have been almost forgotten. One such is Eva Luckes, who dedicated most of her life to nursing here. She was appointed Matron at the relatively young age of 26 in 1880 and introduced changes for 'probationer' (nowadays 'student') nurses which increased their period of training from one to three years, and included classroom training and examinations. She was mentored during this process by Florence Nightingale, with whom she established a strong friendship. Luckes continued in her position of Matron for thirty-nine years, dying in office, and she is remembered by a plaque in the grounds of the medical school and an entrance door on Stepney Way, named in her memory.

Eva Luckes trained many eminent nurses but one in particular, Edith Cavell, is commemorated by a Blue Plaque seen by an entrance door to the old building. Edith worked behind the enemy lines in Brussels, under German Army occupation during the First World War, treating soldiers of all nationalities. Cavell and her colleagues helped over 200 Allied soldiers to escape from German-occupied Belgium but she was eventually arrested and tried by a German military tribunal. Found guilty of 'assisting the enemy' she was executed at dawn by firing squad on 12 October 1915. The Blue Plaque, a nearby street name and an entrance to the new building commemorate her memory.

The authors both contend that perhaps the best kept secret in Whitechapel is that of the Royal London Hospital Museum, located in the crypt of St Augustine with St Philip's Church, Newark Street. Within the museum, you will find a replica of the skeleton of Joseph Merrick (the 'Elephant Man') with documentation about his life at The London (*see* entry No. 26) and fascinating exhibits charting the history of the hospital from its inception until the modern day. No exploration of the centre of Whitechapel is complete without a visit to the museum.

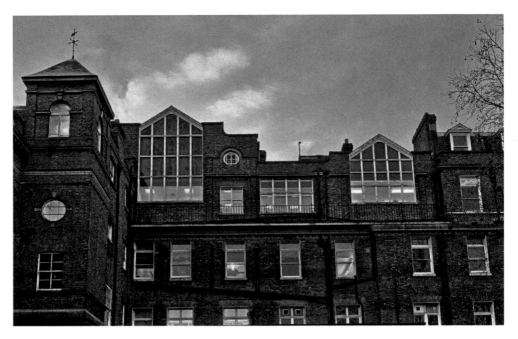

Operating theatre windows, photographed in 2008 when the old hospital was still in use.

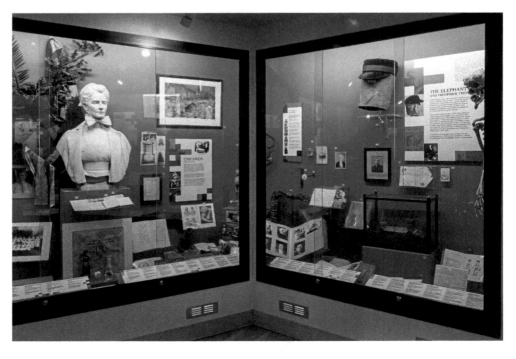

Royal London Hospital Museum: a bust of Edith Cavell (left) and the famous hood of the Elephant Man (right) are on display.

# 25. Alexandra: 'The London's Princess'

On Stepney Way, at the back of the new Royal London Hospital building, stands a majestic bronze statue of Queen Alexandra. She is instantly recognisable, dressed in her coronation robes and holding a sceptre in her right hand. Her hair is coiffed in an

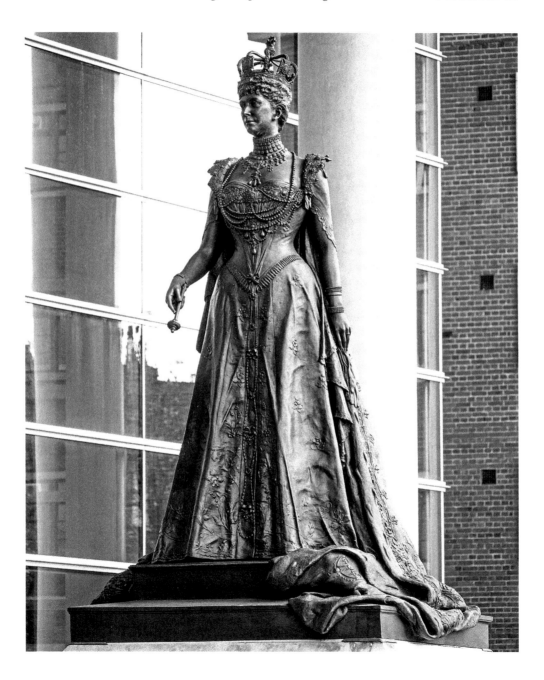

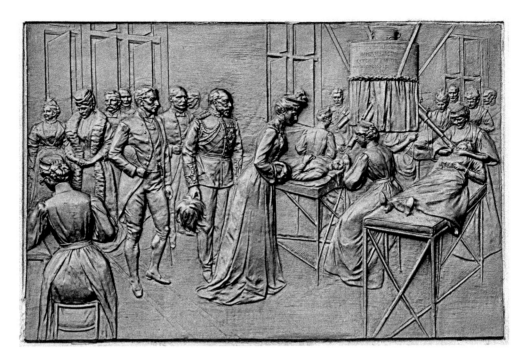

*Previous and above*: The statue of Queen Alexandra, and relief detail of the Finsen Lamp.

up-do and her trademark wide set of stringed pearls adorns her neck. It is said she wore such pearls to hide the scar from a childhood riding accident. Aged over 60 at the time of unveiling in 1908, the statue is realistic as she retained her slim figure throughout her life.

Commissioned by Friends of the Hospital and commemorating her Presidency of the hospital between 1904 and 1908, a relief at the back of the plinth depicts her and her husband, Edward, peering at a hospital bed where a patient is undergoing a new form of ultraviolet light treatment for lupus (an auto-immune condition), the Finsen Lamp. Invented by Dr Niels Finsen in 1899, it won him the Nobel Prize for Medicine in 1903. Alexandra, Danish by birth, beseeched the hospital to view his pioneering work and she subsequently funded the UK's first Finsen Lamp at the London Hospital in 1900. It proved very successful, treating over 100 patients a day for over twenty years, and from the 1920s also treated rickets.

To date Alexandra is the longest-standing Princess of Wales, waiting thirty-nine years before becoming Queen. She had five children in six years, retained her dignity regarding her husband's affairs, and devoted herself to charitable work, notably for nursing children for whom she had genuine concern.

She was particularly fond of the London Hospital and, in 1864, just a year after her marriage to Edward, Prince of Wales, she visited for the first time, opening a childrens' and maternity ward. The same year her husband laid the foundation stone for a new wing to be named in her honour. In 1902, the Queen Alexandra's Imperial Military Nursing

Service was established, later becoming the Queen Alexandra's Royal Army Nursing Corps (the QAs) in 1949. Other hospitals with her name include the National Hospital at Queen Square, where Alexandra House contains neuroscience research units, and Queen Alexandra's Military Hospital, opened in 1905 at Millbank. It closed in 1977 and the site is now used by Tate Britain.

Following her marriage in 1863 numerous streets, artisan cottages and pubs were named in her honour including The Alexandra public house in Wimbledon, near an Alexandra Road, one of an estimated sixty-five roads in London named after her. Among the many buildings commemorating her are Alexandra Cottages in Penge, the Alexandra Trust Dining Rooms, Alexandra House behind the Royal Albert Hall, and Alexandra Palace, affectionately known as 'Ally Pally'.

In 1912, to commemorate the golden jubilee of her arrival in England, she established Alexandra Rose Day, raising money for lesser-known charities. It was the day chosen in 1932 to unveil a dramatic Art Nouveau memorial in St James's symbolising her philanthropy and love of children.

## 26. The 'Penny Gaff' and the Elephant Man

A 'penny gaff' was a Victorian sideshow or entertainment normally in a public house or a disused shop. The name derives from the entrance fee, which was normally one penny.

Today, No. 259 Whitechapel Road (originally No. 123), is an Indian clothing shop in the bustling market but in November 1884 it was a disused grocery shop which had been taken over temporarily by showman, Tom Norman, for his special exhibit.

This exhibit was a man so deformed by an unknown disease that his misshapen head and distorted, grossly enlarged right arm looked like the trunk of an Elephant, hence the crude promotion by the 'gaff' as 'The Elephant Man'. By 1880, this kind of pop-up entertainment had largely disappeared and indeed it attracted the attention of the local police, who closed it down on grounds of public decency.

This was not before 'The Elephant Man' was seen by a student of Dr Frederic Treves, who worked opposite at the London Hospital (*see* entry No. 24) as a surgeon and teacher. The student encouraged his teacher to see the individual for himself.

Frederick described how he found the subject sitting on a stool behind a curtain in a quiet and dejected state, his body covered by a blanket and warming himself on the flame of a simple Bunsen burner. He had come face-to-face with Joseph (aka John) Merrick. Joseph suffered from a condition which grew large clumps of skin and bony protuberances on his body. Even today there is no clear understanding of exactly what caused this condition and it has been subject to much investigation by doctors and biologists.

Born in Leicester in 1862, his condition developed from an early age; he spent time in a workhouse and later worked. In 1884, as his body distorted further, he contacted a showman and moved to London, where he ended up in Norman's grim enterprise.

Frederick was naturally intrigued by what caused this condition and admitted Joseph to The London Hospital for examination. It is claimed that it was Frederick who invented the cap with the full-face veil which Joseph used from that time onwards to hide his face

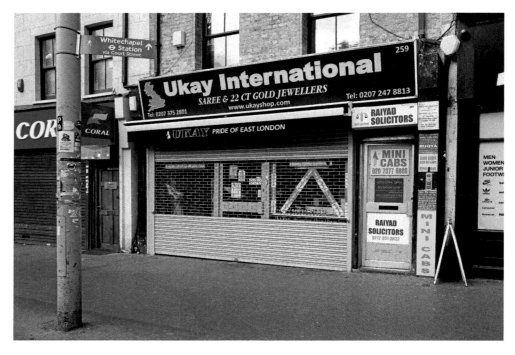

*Above*: No. 259 Whitechapel Road.

*Below left*: A 'carte de visite' of Joseph Merrick when he was living at the London Hospital. (Public Domain)

*Below right*: Sir Frederick Treves, surgeon and friend of Joseph Merrick. (Public Domain)

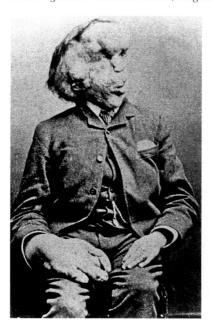

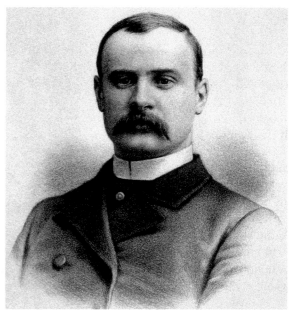

in public. After a brief period, Joseph discharged himself as he felt that he had gone from one form of exhibition to another, this time for the benefit of medical curiosity. When he left the hospital, Frederick pressed on him one of his visiting cards, which a few years later was to quite literally save his life.

For two years, Merrick roamed the continent but was abandoned and eventually found at Liverpool Street station in June 1886. Already drawing crowds and in fear of his life the police once again intervened and, on finding the calling card of Frederick Treves in his pocket, put Joseph into a hansom cab and sent him to The London.

Frederick found Joseph a permanent place in the hospital and he was to stay there until his death in 1890, aged 27. Frederick's own account is heavily romanticised but it is without doubt that he formed a bond with Joseph and it is said he visited him each day. He may have understood him better than anyone else in Joseph's short and difficult life. Accounts support the portrayal that Joseph became a cause célèbre in Victorian society and Alexandra, Princess of Wales (later Queen, the wife of Edward VII) (*see* entry No. 25) met with him during one of her visits to The London.

In recent years, the story of the Elephant Man has gained almost legendary status with books, plays and films, most notably played by John Hurt and most recently a fictionalised appearance in the popular BBC series *Ripper Street*. For this reason, although he was a son of Leicester, his legend will forever be associated with Whitechapel.

# 27. An Oasis in Whitechapel

The first cemetery established by the Jewish community following the resettlement of 1656 was by the Spanish and Portuguese (*see* entry No. 37). The first Ashkenazi (Jews emanating from northern Europe) cemetery was opened in 1697 in the same area, Mile End, by the Great Synagogue of Duke's Place, and closed in 1853.

On entering this secret and sacred space through the almost unnoticed door within a long brick wall on Alderney Road, visitors are immediately enthralled by the memories of this early community. The cherubs and skulls on some graves are a reminder that they used local stonemasons who had a set range of designs. Jewish rituals and customs from abroad were brought to this new home and none more personified this more than Samuel Falk, who is buried here. The 'Baal Shem (Master of the Name) of London', Falk was a prominent and controversial eighteenth-century figure. He was the leading exponent of Kabbalah, a mystical interpretation of Jewish traditions, and, on moving to London, he enjoyed success as a mystic, amassing great wealth from providing his services, much of which he left to charitable causes after his death.

Also buried at Alderney Road are some of the earliest religious leaders, including Aaron and David Tevele Schiff, the first two Chief Rabbis of the Ashkenazi community.

In 1761, a field in Whitechapel was leased and Brady Street Cemetery was established by another synagogue, The New. This operated as a burial ground for just under 100 years, when by this time it had been used to its capacity.

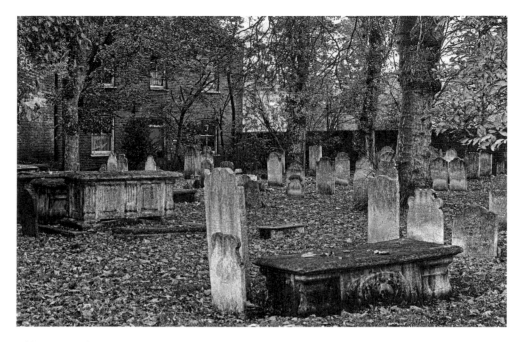

Alderney Road cemetery.

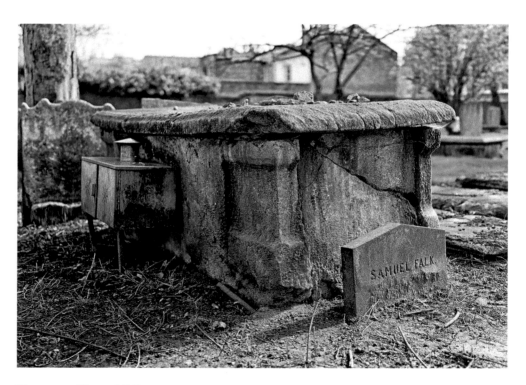

The grave of Samuel Falk.

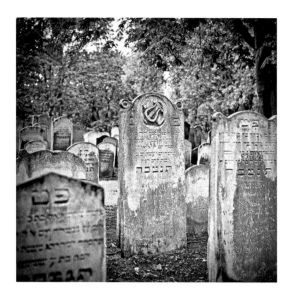 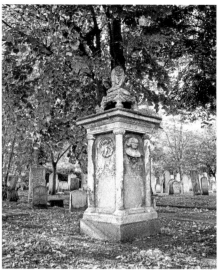

*Above left*: Decorated headstones at Brady Street cemetery.

*Above right*: The memorial to Miriam Levy in Brady Street cemetery.

The significance of Brady Street is that during its lifetime it witnessed great advances in how the Jewish community, and indeed all immigrant communities, were treated in British society. After the Reform Act of 1832, Jews and Catholics could take public office. By the time Brady Street closed in 1858 the first Jewish Lord Mayor of London, David Salomons, had been elected in 1855 and the first official Jewish MP, Lionel de Rothschild, had taken his seat in 1858. As such, the history of the cemetery at Brady Street is part of the story of the Anglo-Jewish community itself.

The cemetery contains the graves of individuals from a broad spectrum. At one end there are the artisan workers, such as carters and shipbuilders, while at the other, it is the resting place of Nathaniel Rothschild and Joseph Hambro, both of whom created financial institutions still evident in the City today. In addition to the humble and the great there is also an unusual memorial to a woman, Miriam Levy.

Her memorial is unique as the structure incorporates a bust, presumably of Miriam herself. It is very rare for the human form to be depicted on Jewish gravestones. Despite the obvious lavish memorial to someone who must have been much loved and significant, there is very little information about who Miriam was. It is believed she may have established the first soup kitchen in the East End for Jewish poor.

As closed cemeteries, both Alderney Road and Brady Street have over the years been slowly reverting to nature. In particular, Brady Street during the summer months seems more like a forest than a cemetery and all year round provides a much-needed refuge for wildlife from the heavily urbanised environment surrounding the grounds.

Both cemeteries are open only by appointment through the United Synagogue (theus.org.uk).

# 28. Academy to Army

No. 23 New Road is a handsome Georgian house. It bears a Tower Hamlets Environment Trust plaque proclaiming, 'The first indoor meeting of the mission which was to become The Salvation Army was held here on 3rd September 1865'.

The founder of the Salvation Army was William Booth, a former pawnbroker turned Methodist preacher. He arrived in London in 1865 and began preaching on Whitechapel Waste, just east of the Mile End tollgate, where today statues of William and his wife Catherine are found. History records he was popular with the crowds and was invited to continue his mission in a tent on a nearby former Quaker burial ground, now Vallance Gardens (*see* entry No. 20). At the time, Booth's movement was called the East London Christian Mission, which he renamed the Salvation Army in 1878.

His tent was old and torn and, with a growing set of adherents to his cause, Booth sought out premises in which to hold his services and meetings. The first such meeting took place here in the incongruously named 'Professor Orson's Dancing Academy', although the building was in fact called the Assembly Rooms. The main room was large enough to accommodate dancing and thus could hold large crowds for evangelical meetings.

The building was rented out at various times to different users and even on a Sunday Booth had to contend with others using the premises.

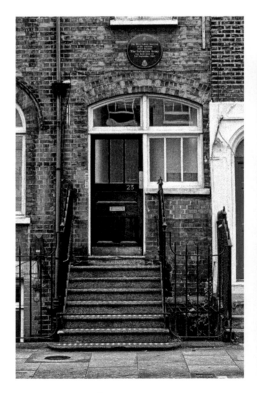 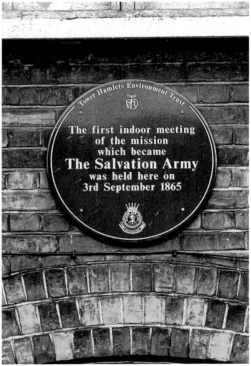

No. 23 New Road.

Not unsurprisingly, a lot more is known about Booth's life than that of Professor Orson. William and his wife were already a formidable team when they set up their Mission in London. In addition to religious evangelism, the Salvation Army was committed to helping the socially disadvantaged. Its initiatives included rescue work, maternity homes, a model match factory, brass bands and international activity. It spread the word through its journal, *The War Cry*, and promoted equality between its men and women members.

Today, the Salvation Army works in over 125 countries and this early Mission site is now divided into flats.

## 29. Tommy Flowers

Henriques Street contains an educational establishment which in recent years has been renamed the Tommy Flowers Centre. The school began life in 1903 as the Berners Street Combined Special School. Today, this would be the equivalent of providing vocational training courses. In 1903, these included cookery and laundry and in 1909 the Manual Training Centre (MTC) was added. The school was a pioneering establishment recognising, as now, that some children require additional support to gain skills for their adult lives.

The building is one of the most attractive London School Board buildings of its era, with is cupola-topped tower built of red brick and Portland stone. Many original features

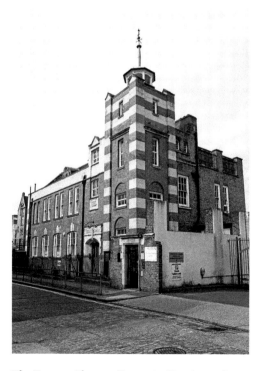
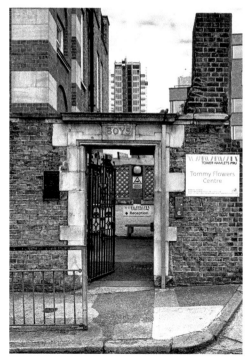

The Tommy Flowers Centre in Henriques Street.

remain such as the ornate ironwork railings and the signage for 'Boys', 'Cookery and Laundry', 'MTC' and 'Girls'.

In the early part of the 2010s, the building was used for the City Learning Centre, an ambitious attempt to offer IT-related learning courses to all levels of students. It was renamed the Tommy Flowers Centre but eventually closed through lack of funding. The choice of the new name recognised one of the most important sons of the London Borough of Tower Hamlets, Tommy Flowers, who oversaw the development of something so top secret that in his lifetime he was barely acknowledged.

During the Second World War, the Government Code and Ciphers School (later GCHQ) read encrypted enemy signals at Bletchley Park, a highly classified location in Buckinghamshire. Much is now known about the work there but it was not until the 1970s that the activities were openly discussed.

History concentrated on the work of Alan Turing breaking the Enigma code machines used by the German Army and Navy to encrypt messages. However, there was an even more difficult cipher in use, the Lorenz code machines, concealing messages between the highest echelons of the German armed forces. William Tutte cracked the code but it was Tommy Flowers from Poplar and a senior electrical engineer with the General Post Office who devised a switching device, Colossus. This accelerated the code breaking at Bletchley Park. This device has now been recognised as one of the earliest electronic computers ever built but, due to the constraints of wartime secrecy, it was not acknowledged until many years later. Indeed, after the war Flowers sought finance for a commercial computer but his proposals were rejected as not being credible!

Despite an MBE for efforts unrelated to Colossus, there is little evidence of Flower's life in the public domain. The road containing the Dollis Hill research station was renamed in his honour after his death in 1998, aged 93, and the IT department of Swanlea School, Whitechapel contains a 'Tommy Flowers Zone'. Although the City Learning Centre has closed, it's chosen name, the Tommy Flowers Centre, remains as a centre to help Year 11 students struggling with mainstream school; an initiative that a self-made boy from East London, like Tommy, would surely applaud.

## 30. The Mortuary That Became a Nature Study Centre

In the south-east corner of St George's Gardens, Cable Street, in the former churchyard of St George in the East, designed by Nicholas Hawksmoor, is a small derelict structure built as a mortuary in 1876.

The need for mortuaries starts with the realisation in early Victorian London of a rather grisly practice. As London grew, families living in one room might also live with their 'dearly departed' for some time before affording or arranging burial.

Churchyards, sufficient for a small local population, ran out of space during the rapid Victorian urbanisation and while large municipal cemeteries were established, they were some distance from the parishes. Transporting the dead to these new cemeteries also led to delays in burial.

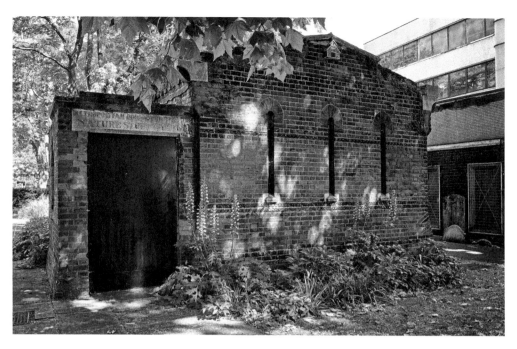

The mortuary at St George's in the East.

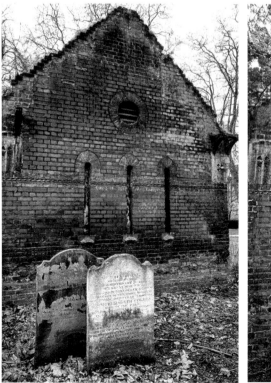

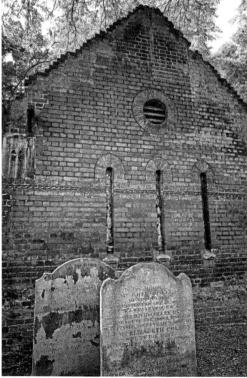

From 1866, legislation allowed magistrates to insist that bodies be removed and placed in a mortuary for post-mortems and to control the spread of infectious diseases. However, parishes were not compelled to create mortuaries and there was considerable public resistance regarding the treatment and respect bodies would receive during their repose. The lingering fear about body snatchers also remained even though by the 1870s this practise had ceased. Such reasons may have delayed the establishment of a mortuary here until the 1870s.

This mortuary is classic Victorian gothic with wonderful ornamental detail. The brick building was single storey, with an entrance vestibule and two rooms covered by a wooden roof, now largely destroyed. The alternate layers of different coloured brickwork with lines of terracotta tiles create an intricate pattern, and terracotta V-shape friezes surround the main ventilation slits. Perhaps, the (sadly unknown) architect was attempting to complement the brilliance of Hawksmoor's church with a fine building worthy of being in its shadow.

Inside, the walls of the infectious diseases room were covered with beautiful cream-glazed tiles, the height of sanitary hygiene at the time.

The mortuary gained fame in 1888 through the Whitechapel Murders, following the discovery in the early hours of Sunday 30 September of the mutilated body of Elizabeth 'Long Liz' Stride in nearby Berner Street (now Henriques Street). Her body was brought here for a post-mortem, which established on the Monday that the mutilations were like those of two murdered women discovered during the previous four weeks. The inquest itself was opened in the Vestry Hall, Cable Street later the same day.

The murder created a sensation throughout the East End, and indeed the whole country because less than an hour after Elizabeth's body was discovered another victim, Catherine Eddowes, was discovered on the edge of Whitechapel in Mitre Square.

By the turn of the century, purpose-built morgues using refrigeration to store bodies for extended periods had eclipsed the use of mortuaries and St George's was closed.

However, in 1904 the building began a new lease of life, being converted into the Metropolitan Borough of Stepney Nature Study Museum. This provided children with the opportunity to see specimens of natural history (including, it is reported, a live monkey) and bringing the countryside into the city, a precursor to London's City Farms (*see* entry No. 17). By all accounts, it was a great success and was visited regularly by school groups and children during their holidays. As the Second World War began and children were evacuated, the museum struggled on but eventually closed its doors in 1942.

Sadly, since that time it has been left to deteriorate, although it is a testament to the original Victorian builders that the main structure is still sound. It has been the subject of several proposals to refurbish it and bring it back into use, which would be a marvellous extension to an already extraordinary life.

# 31. The Siege of Sidney Street

Peter House and Painter House stand at the southern end of Sidney Street. Built in 2006–08 by Tower Hamlets Community Housing, the names link to one of the most notorious crimes of the early twentieth century, as does Siege House further up the road.

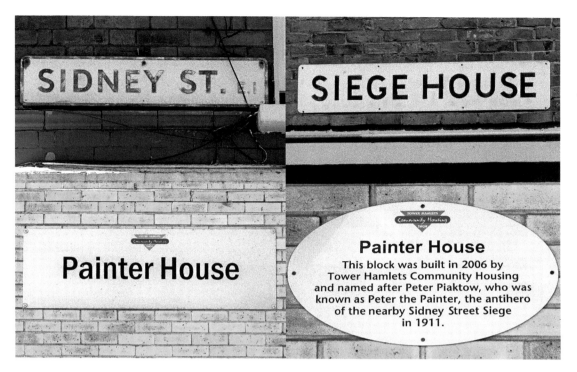

Sidney Street signs.

During a bungled burglary on 16 December 1910 at Exchange Buildings, Houndsditch, three policemen were killed and the burglars took flight. They were believed to be eastern European anarchists, as such a crime could not be 'English'. One assailant, Latvian George Gardstein (*see* entry No. 14) had been shot during the gun-fight and later died in their hideout in Grove Street, where radical literature found seemed to confirm their anarchist origins.

Despite a wide search they were not found but in January 1911 they were recognised by a Mrs Gershon, who rented a room to them at No. 100 Sidney Street. Neighbours were evacuated from their homes and police and the Scots Guards surrounded the premises. With the Horse Artillery on alert, the siege began on 2 January 1911. The Home Secretary, Winston Churchill, in a fur-collared coat and top hat, was in attendance and hundreds of locals waited for the action to begin. On 3 January shots rang out, the building went up in smoke and two bodies were found. Peter Piatkov (known as Peter the Painter), a famous anarchist, was expected to be a third victim but he seemingly disappeared and speculation continues to this day.

In 1960 a film was made with Dublin standing in for Whitechapel, the original house having been demolished in 1956 and the new building on the site named Siege House.

The definitive version of events was written by Professor William Fishman in his book *East End Radicals*, and artefacts used in the burglary and the police investigation are on display at the City of London Police Museum.

# 32. The Father of Bangladesh

In the front garden of one of Erlich Cottages (post-war homes on Sidney Street) stands a handsome brass statuette of the Bangladeshi statesman and politician, Sheikh Mujibur Rahman. Known as the 'Father of Bangladesh', Mujibur was considered the driving force in the independence movement which split the former East Pakistan from control, at the time, by West Pakistan. After independence, as Bangladesh, he served as its first President but was assassinated, together with his family, during a coup d'état in 1975.

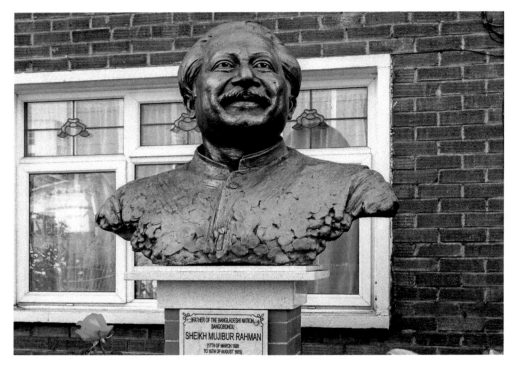

The statue of Sheik Mujibur Rahman in Sidney Street.

## DID YOU KNOW?

When the London Borough of Stepney (later part of the London Borough of Tower Hamlets) was naming newly built post-war homes they often chose the surnames of local residents who had died during the Blitz. Erlich Cottages commemorate David and Lotte Ehrlich of No. 85 Stepney Way, who were killed in September 1941, and Ansell House, just behind, remembers Frederick and Lucy Ansell of No. 49 Wilkes Street, Spitalfields, both killed in May 1941.

Bangladesh remembers his birthday each year as a public holiday and a museum in his memory was established at the Dhaka home where he was killed.

The large Bengali community in Whitechapel explains the siting of the statue in this area. Unveiled in December 2016 on Bangladesh Victory Day, the 16th, which commemorates victory over West Pakistan, the statue was commissioned by the Awami League, a political group for British Bangladeshis. The statue, the first made of Mujibar, was unveiled by Suranjit Sen, a Bangladeshi MP, outside the home of Awami League Joint Secretary.

# 33. Challahs to Crodoughs

The face of a distinguished looking gentleman with a handlebar moustache looks out from the north side of Rinkoff's café on Vallance Road. He arrived on this brick wall in the early 2000s and is a wonderful example of a style of adverts once seen all over London, using walls to advertise goods and services. Early examples, mostly faded or repainted, linked to businesses now closed, are known as ghost signs, but he is no ghost. This gentleman is found again alongside Rinkoff's bakery on O'Leary Square. He is Hyman Rinkoff, a Ukranian who moved to London in 1906 and in 1911 founded his family bakery business in Old Montague Street, near Black Lion Yard (now Black Lion House).

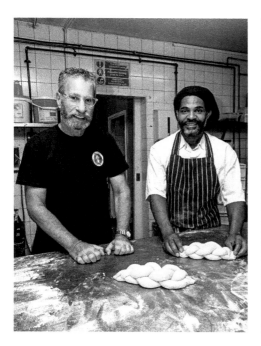 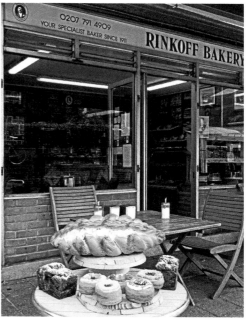

*Above left*: Ray Rinkoff and Richard Watts platting the challah dough.

*Above right*: Challah and crodoughs.

The bakery remained there until 1971, when a compulsory purchase order necessitated a move. It did not go far away, opening in O'Leary Square opposite Jubilee Street and Adelina Grove. The café in Vallace Road opened in 1978, where the corner site has been selling bagels since the 1940s. Several different bakeries occupied this spot with Rinkoff succeeding the famous Blue and White All Night.

Hyman's grandson, Ray, joined the family business in 1968 and still works there with fourth generation Rinkoffs, Lloyd and Jennifer, He has seen some big changes. Sunday is no longer the busiest day. Back in the 1970s, the Sunday queues snaked around the block and, from being 95 per cent retail business, is now 70 per cent wholesale, with top department stores Selfridges and Harrods among the clients. Keeping up with fast-moving tastes in bread and pastries, Rinkoff's invented the London version of the Cronut, a delicious combination of a croissant and doughnut they named the Crodough. They also bake the rainbow bagel, celebrating the LGBT community, but there are still the staple Danish pastries, filled bagels and challahs (sweet plaited bread made with egg eaten by Jewish families on the Sabbath and festivals) to enjoy.

Rinkoff's was not the first Jewish baker in the East End to gain fame throughout the Jewish community. Grodzinski has that honour, being founded in 1888 on Cavell Street (then Bedford Street) near the London Hospital before moving to Fieldgate Street. In 1930, they opened a second bakery in Dunsmure Road, Stamford Hill, which became the main bakery when Fieldgate Street was destroyed during the Blitz. 'Grods' is still family owned with branches in London's Jewish suburbs. Other Jewish bakers include Kossoff's but it is Rinkoffs, still in Whitechapel, that has stood the test of East End time.

For all these bakers life was hard work. The working day began at 3 a.m. when the ovens were lit, and bagel bakers could work for over eighteen hours a day with a daily rate of between 1/9d and 2/6d. The London Jewish Bakers' Union was founded in 1905 following an unsuccessful 1904 strike which demanded a twelve-hour day, restricted overtime and a minimum wage of 26/- per week. By the 1920s, there were 120 union members working for thirty-five bakeries. With 150 members at its height, by the late 1960s only twelve remained and the union closed in 1970, ending its days as the longest lasting Jewish union. Regular strikes, particularly one in 1913, brought reduced hours, increased pay and union recognition, and people were encouraged to buy union bread, supporting bakeries

## DID YOU KNOW?

Founded in 1974, the Brick Lane Beigel Bakery bakes bagels (or beigels) the traditional way, boiling the dough before baking, which gives bagels their crispy crust protecting the fluffy white dough inside. Open 24 hours a day every day of the year, between 2,000 and 3,000 bagels are baked each day, with salt beef and pickle now the most requested filling, ousting the long-established favourite, smoked salmon and cream cheese.

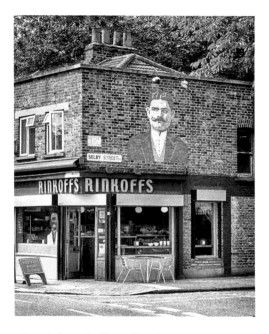

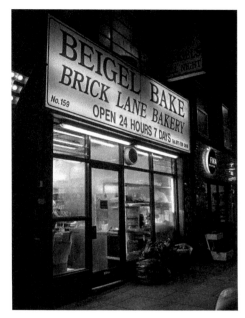

*Above left*: Rinkoff's Café at the corner of Vallance Road and Selby Street.

*Above right*: Brick Lane Beigel Bake.

that treated their employees decently. A large painted silk banner for the London Jewish Bakers' Union is on display at the Jewish Museum in Camden Town. Dating from around 1925, one side is in English, showing worker solidarity, a loaf of Union Bread and a plaited challah, with the other side depicting the message in Yiddish.

## 34. Mercers' Maidens

Exploring London provides many hints to land ownership past and present. Landowning families or City Livery Companies are commemorated in street and building names or maybe coats of arms adorning stonework. But the most delightful indicators to land ownership are surely the Mercers' Maidens.

Sometimes modestly clothed, sometimes less so, sometimes painted, sometimes in natural stone, only the maidens' top half is ever portrayed. They are the symbol of the Mercers, the premier Livery Company, and they grace documents and official furniture and indicate property owned by them. There are over 100 Maidens to seek out in London alone and several are in Whitechapel.

City Livery Companies developed from trade guilds and now number 110. An order of precedence was set in 1515 for the forty-eight Companies then in existence and the Mercers were allocated top position. Companies were responsible for administering apprenticeships and ensuring quality control of their particular products. They also

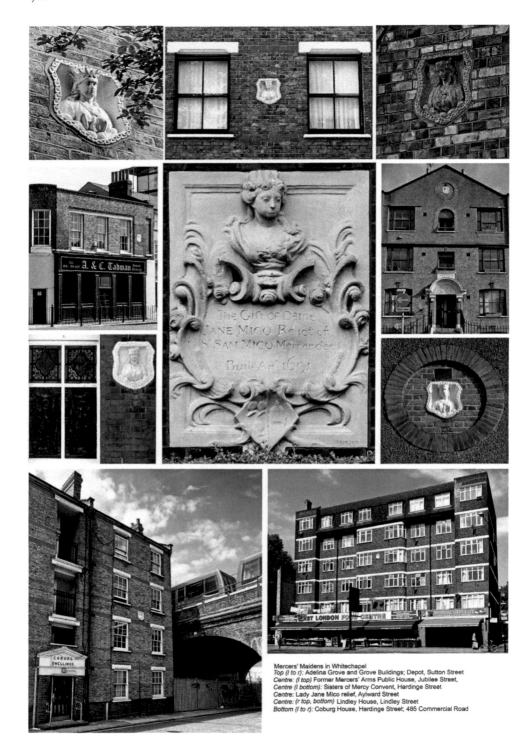

Mercers' Maidens in Whitechapel
*Top (l to r):* Adelina Grove and Grove Buildings; Depot, Sutton Street
*Centre: (l top)* Former Mercers' Arms Public House, Jubilee Street,
*Centre (l bottom):* Sisters of Mercy Convent, Hardinge Street
*Centre:* Lady Jane Mico relief, Aylward Street
*Centre: (r top, bottom)* Lindley House, Lindley Street
*Bottom (l to r):* Coburg House, Hardinge Street; 485 Commercial Road

Mercers' Maidens in Whitechapel.

provided almshouses for elderly members or widows, funded educational establishments and established charitable trusts.

Although City institutions, the Companies could own property anywhere and the Mercers acquired land in Whitechapel as early as the 1500s. In 1690, they built almshouses for eight elderly women opposite the church of St Dunstan, Stepney, funded by a legacy from Lady Jane Mico, widow of mercer Sir Samuel Mico. They became known as Lady Mico's Almshouses, were rebuilt in 1856 and relocated in 1976 to new premises on Aylward Street, providing homes for nineteen single women together with a resident warden. A stone Maiden from the original almshouses was placed on the new exterior.

The original almshouses were acquired by Greater London Council (GLC) as part of the property exchange and have been private residences since 1970. An ornate stone Maiden remains in situ.

On Grove Dwellings, Adelina Grove, near the junction with Jubilee Street, Maidens are seen on a group of two-storey homes built in 1910 on land leased from the Mercers, which was previously used for a dairy and small factory.

Other Maidens found in the area include those on pubs (York Square and Jubilee Street), offices (Arbour Square), a mission on Commercial Road and residences in Lindley and Hardinge Streets.

The earliest Maidens date from seals at the time of their second Charter of 1425 but despite speculation, it is not known why or when the Mercers originally chose the Maiden as their emblem nor why they are only ever shown from the waist up. Despite speculation, her origins remain a mystery.

Several Mercers' Maidens are also found in the City of London, easily reached from the East End, and in Covent Garden you can find Maidens in Mercer Street, named to indicate land owned by the Mercers Company.

The Mercers continue the traditions of the past with both a charitable and educational trust endowing several schools including St Paul's, administering Gresham College, running the Mercers' Company Housing Association and providing almshouses linked to the Whittington Charity, a trust established by one of the most famous mercers, Richard (Dick) Whittington, four times Lord Mayor of the City of London.

# 35. A Nest of Gentle Anarchists

Dunstan Houses at the north end of Stepney Green is a solid red brick block of flats decorated with cupolas at the corners and wrought ironwork on the stairwells. Now part social and part private housing, it was built in 1899 by the East End Dwellings Company founded by Samuel Barnett in 1882. It proved an inspiration to Lord Rothschild whose 4 Per Cent Industrial Dwelling Company's Stepney Green Dwellings (now Court) at the southern end of Stepney Green is the oldest surviving example of 4 Per Cent blocks (see entry No. 8).

The East End Dwellings differed from other philanthropic housing in that the casual poor and day labourers were allowed to live there as well as those on regular, if low, incomes. East End Dwellings Company buildings are still found all over London although the first, Katharine Buildings in Aldgate, built in 1885, has been demolished.

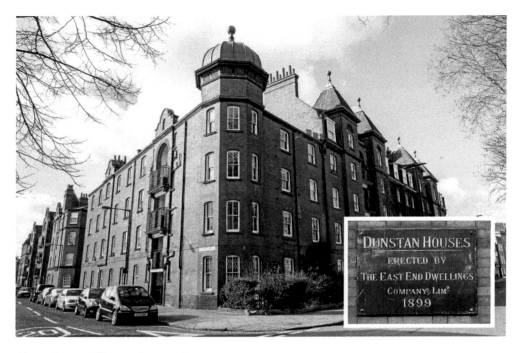

*Above*: Dunstan Houses, Stepney Green.

*Below*: Rudolph Rocker (back row, second left) and Millie Witcop (front row, left). (© The Jewish Museum)

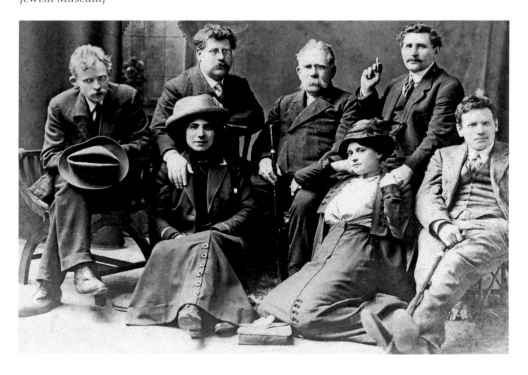

Survivors include Wentworth Buildings in Whitechapel, Merceron and Gretton Houses in Bethnal Green and Thornhill House in Islington. All were designed using red brick and incorporated towers, gables and domes, as seen at Dunstan Houses. Health and hygiene were paramount, together with a sense of responsibility for the tenants to pay rent on time, mirroring the ethos of Octavia Hill, the pioneer of housing management a few decades earlier.

Flat 33 was home to Rudolph Rocker, where he lived in free union with his Jewish partner Millie Witcop. In 1895, Rudolph, German born, Christian and orphaned, arrived in London

## DID YOU KNOW?

### Best for Health

At No. 4, Stepney Green a renovated ghost sign for Daren Bread prompts memories of a once well-known brand across the nation. Made with additive-free whole-wheat flour ground from Daren Mill on the River Darent in Dartford, Kent, it was promoted as a healthy alternative to white loaves. In the 1930s, it was taken over by its main competitor, Hovis, and by the early 1960s the brand was forgotten, although many Daren ghost signs remain throughout the UK.

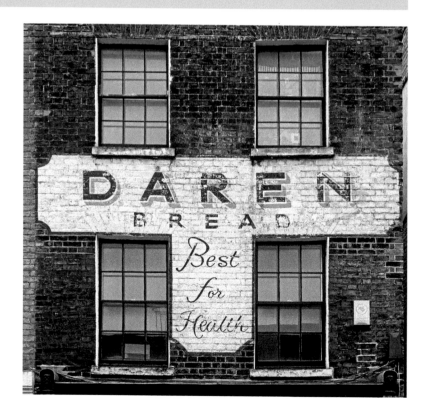

Daren Bread ghost sign.

having moved across Europe, escaping arrest for his anarchist views. In East London with its working-class population, many of whom were Jewish, he found his spiritual home. He was soon invited to edit the Yiddish newspaper *Dos Freie Vort* (The Free Word) so learnt Yiddish and eventually edited *Arbeiter Freund* (Workers Friend) and Germinal.

The flat became an informal HQ for the European anarchist community. Many, like Rudolph, had escaped arrest and his visitors included Errico Malatesta, seen with Rudolph on the Anarchists' Mural (*see* entry No. 14).

In 1902, Rudolph encouraged the formation of a federation of Jewish anarchist clubs, named the Arbeiter Freund Club and Institute. In 1906, its HQ was established at No. 165 Jubilee Street (now demolished), where it became central to social, trade union and intellectual activities.

He encouraged Jewish artisans to unionise and support their fellow workers, Jewish and non-Jewish. When in 1912, both dockers and the West End tailors went on strike Rudolph encouraged the Jewish community to support both strikes. When over 13,000 East End garment workers joined the 7,000 West End tailors already on strike, their demands were soon met. As the dockers' strike dragged, on the Jewish community did all they could to assist, feeding the dockers' children and providing accommodation. Eventually, this strike too was a success.

Rudolph and Millie were anti-war but in 1914 he was arrested as an enemy alien and interned throughout the First World War at Alexandra Palace, Olympia, and on the *Prince Edward* prison ship. He never saw his Dunstan Houses home again. Millie was also arrested for her pacifist views. The Jewish anarchist movement never fully recovered and most of its members became Zionists or communists.

After the war, Rudolph and Millie were deported to Holland. They moved to Germany but with the rise of Nazism in the 1930s escaped to America.

The irony is that in 1897 Rudolph and Millie travelled to America for work, registering as married for the voyage. On arriving at Ellis Island, they were asked for their marriage certificate and responded by explaining that their bond was one of free agreement. Millie further explained that she did not consider it dignified to hold a man's love purely by the power of law. When told that 'if everyone ignored the law in respect of marriage, we should have free love' Millie's reply was, 'Love is always free. When love ceases to be free, it is prostitution.'

They refused to marry legally and returned to London. America's loss was the East End's gain.

# 36. Whitechapel Hideaways

Whitechapel, despite widespread slum clearance after the Second World War, expansive social housing estates and contemporary steel and glass tower blocks, still retains some delightful alleyways and courtyards that somehow have escaped the developers' demolition ball.

Behind Wickhams (the grand department store on Mile End Road which at the time of writing is being redeveloped into an upmarket banqueting venue and retail centre) lies Belle Vue Place.

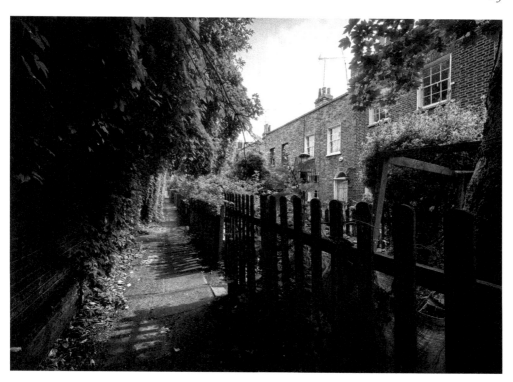

*Above*: Belle Vue Place.

*Right*: Anchor Brewery relief.

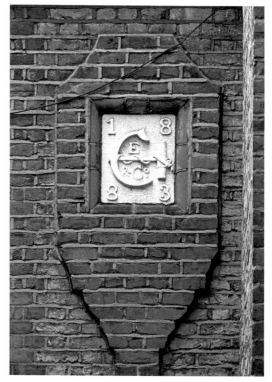

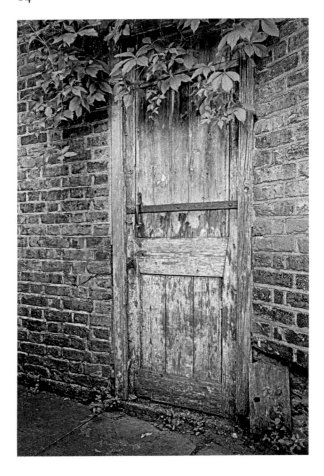

Shortcut to the Brewery.

It is easy to miss the tiny entrance where a wooden door leads to a secret garden with a row of early nineteenth-century flat-fronted cottages, seemingly unchanged for centuries. The front gardens in summer are a riot of colour with roses, clematis and lilac joining the winding creepers behind wooden picket fences.

Originally it was a crescent with a communal green used as a tea garden but when Charrington's built its Anchor brewery, the terrace was cut in half and the brewery rented the cottages to their workers. As recently as the 1990s, it still owned a third of the homes. A doorway led to the brewery complex (perhaps to ensure prompt arrival for work) and that still exists albeit locked. An ornate plaque depicting an anchor remains. Despite having outside toilets and just two bedrooms, these cottages, known as 'two-up, two-downs', would have been home to families with several children. Past residents reminiscing for the Spitalfields Life blog (spitalfieldslife.com), remembered the many joint parties and celebrations and the safe environment for children to enjoy. As everyone worked together at the brewery there was an additional sense of community and, of course, a ready supply of freshly brewed alcohol! The brewery also arranged for No. 1, larger than the others, to be converted into an informal social centre.

In the mid-1950s, locals nicknamed it 'Bunghole Alley' and much preferred the luxury of a flat in the new post-war Ocean Estate. Today, the residents are more likely to be barristers, IT consultants and designers, representing the changing demographics of the area and the property prices reinforce the story, having risen seven-fold in two decades.

The special quality of this secluded spot was recognised as far back as 1962, and Geoffrey Fletcher included it in his book *The London Nobody Knows*, where he wrote about hidden gems of London and for the third edition in 1996 his illustration of Belle Vue Place graced the cover.

Further east off the Mile End Road through a dilapidated arch lies Mile End Place. It is not so hidden as Belle Vue Place and the cottages are slightly smaller but it also remains a quiet enclave of early nineteenth-century cottages built for the local artisan and factory workers.

## DID YOU KNOW?

Frederick Charrington, of the brewing family, established a mission promoting temperance, and in 1886 his Great Assembly Hall was opened on Mile End Road. Bombed during the Second World War, the site is now Tower Hamlets Mission, reopened in 1988 and extended several times with additional flats and facilities. Continuing Frederick's vision Charis and The Terrace provide refuge and practical help for those battling addictions.

# 37. House of Life

The first recorded cemetery for London's Jewish community was situated near Moorgate, and until 1177 was the only one in England. No other Jewish burial grounds were evident in London until the Resettlement of 1656 when Oliver Cromwell allowed Jews back to Britain following their expulsion by King Edward I in 1290. The Sephardi (Spanish and Portuguese) Jews were the first to return, followed swiftly by Ashkenazi (northern European) Jews. Both communities settled just outside the City in Aldgate and quickly established cemeteries further east in Mile End.

The Velho or Old Cemetery is the oldest Jewish cemetery in Britain following the Resettlement and is one of the area's hidden secrets, unseen except from the back windows of Albert Stern House on Mile End Road or through a small wooden door within the campus of Queen Mary University of London (QMUL) (*see* entry No. 38). Opened in 1657, the area was then semi-rural with orchards when local church bells tolled for the first funerals. Plague victims from 1665 were buried there and, as the community grew, the cemetery was extended, but closed in 1735.

Today, it is mostly a grassy field with flat gravestones, many unreadable. Early epitaphs were in Portuguese and occasionally Spanish. Later, Hebrew and English were used and on the north wall is seen a restored plaque from 1684 recording the placing of the first

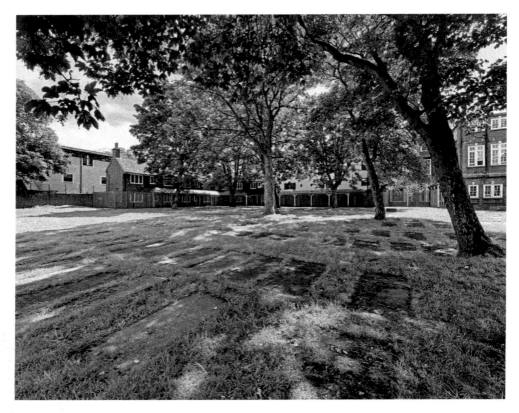

Velho cemetery.

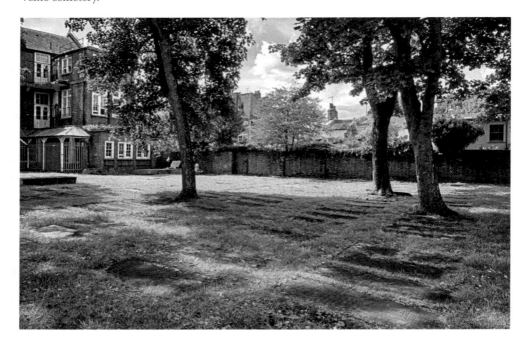

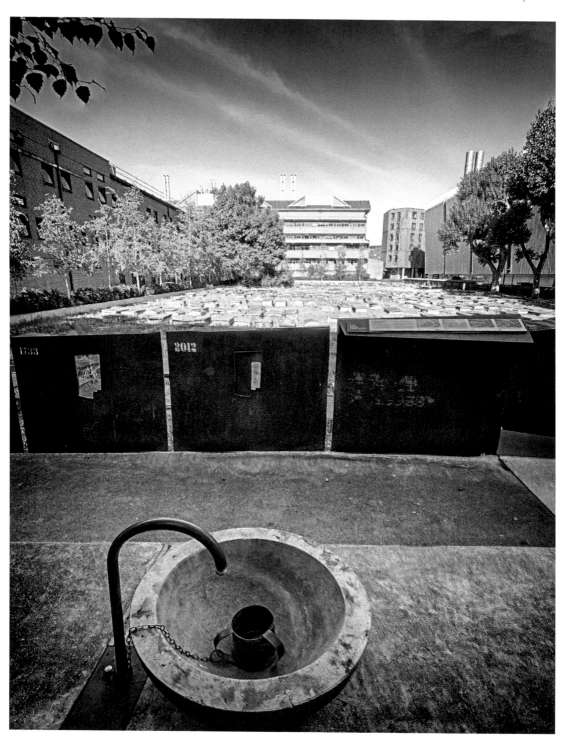

Novo cemetery.

stone. Surrounding the north perimeter is a set of verandaed cottages built in 1913 for married couples living at the Sephardi Old Age Home. Opened in 1747 on Leman Street, in 1790 the home joined provision for the sick and lying-in women on this site since 1665. Rebuilt in 1913 as Albert Stern House the old age home remained here until relocating to Wembley in 1977 and the building was adapted as accommodation for QMUL students. Looking at Albert Stern House from the Mile End Road there is no hint of the cemetery behind.

As the early Sephardi community grew a larger cemetery was needed. Land was bought in 1724 and in 1733 the Novo or New Cemetery opened close to the Velho. Enlarged in the 1850s the cemetery remained in use until 1918 and it officially closed in 1936. Only a fraction of the original cemetery remains.

In 1974, QMUL acquired a large section for their new library and 7,500 graves were reinterred in Brentwood, Essex. Found behind the Arts and Law faculties, the cemetery has recently been sensitively re-landscaped, showcasing the historic graves that remain. Names such as Sassoon and Montefiore resonate to this day and places mentioned on the graves such as Gibraltar, Morocco, South America and Australia illustrate the global nature of the early community. Financier Sampson Gideon was buried here. He had converted to Christianity but continued to pay his burial dues anonymously. He and religious leaders were reinterred at Hoop Lane Cemetery, Golders Green. Opened in 1896 and jointly owned by the Spanish & Portuguese and Reform communities, the first burial was in 1897 and the cemetery still functions today.

There is open access to the Novo, and the Velho can be visited by arrangement by emailing velhocemetery@sephardi.org.uk.

# 38. The People's Palace

Queen Mary University of London (QMUL) stretches from the Regents Canal alongside Mile End Park to beyond Bancroft Road. Over the past few years expansion on the south side of Mile End Road is evident, with student accommodation and union premises. With over 21,000 students, it is the third largest college in the University of London and since 2013 has been granting its own degrees.

The site holds many secrets including two Sephardi Jewish cemeteries (*see* entry No. 37) dating from 1657 and 1733, the wonderful interior of a grand library known as the Octagon, built in 1887, and the People's Palace, opened in 1937. To understand how Queen Mary College developed, the story goes back to 1727 when Francis Bancroft, a member of the Drapers' Company, left a legacy for a school and almshouses, establishing Bancroft's Hospital and School on this site. Nearly 100 years later, in 1841, John Barber Beaumont opened his New Philosophical Institute on Beaumont Square, providing adult education classes. He instructed the Drapers' Company to administer it after his death, which occurred shortly afterwards. In the mid-1880s, the Drapers decided to merge the two legacies. The Beaumont Square premises were vacated and Bancroft School moved to Woodford, Essex liberating the site for the East London Technical College and People's Palace incorporating the Queen's Hall. Providing

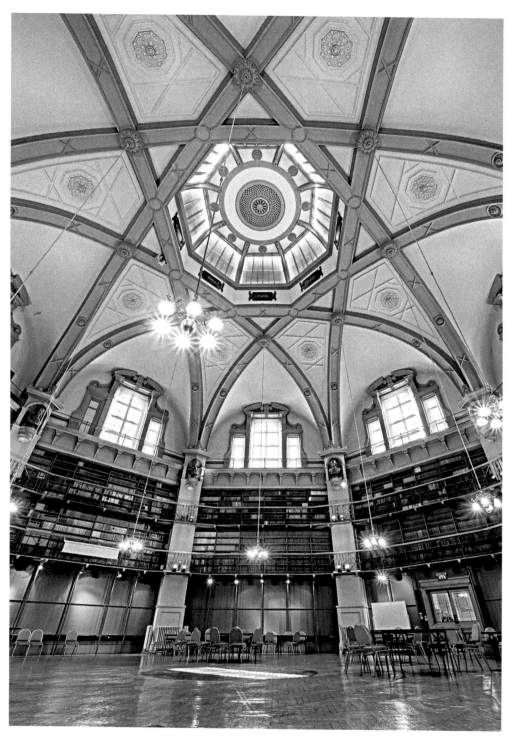

Octagon at Queen Mary University, London.

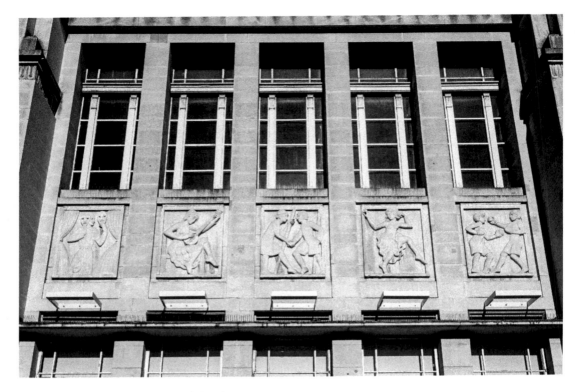

Frieze by Eric Gill at the People's Palace.

both educational and recreational facilities for the local working-class community, it was instantly successful, with exhibitions and shows in the Queen's Hall receiving thousands of visitors. The original frontage from 1887 still stands today.

A public library was also built. Octagonal in shape, it was modelled on the Reading Room of the British Museum with triple-height shelving and glazed lantern at the top bringing in natural light for reading. There was room for 250,000 books, most of which were donated by authors and publishers, and over 1,000 readers used it every day. However, when the new public library opened in Bancroft Road in 1902, the Octagon became superfluous to public needs and was closed. In 1909, it became a hall for recreational activities and from 1920 the main College Library. The interwar years saw a conflict of interest between the educational and recreational facilities and when fire destroyed the Queen's Hall in 1931 it prompted a decision to split the two. A Royal Charter of 1934 confirmed the educational side as Queen Mary College and a new People's Palace for recreation was built alongside, fronting Mile End Road. Opening it in 1937 was King George VI's first public engagement.

The exterior of the People's Palace is decorated with reliefs by Eric Gill, the letterist and sculptor. The handshake depicts Fellowship, the boxers Sport, the masks and stage curtains, Drama, the dancer Dance and a mandolin player, Music. Above the doorways additional reliefs show a musician playing a trumpet and a figure reading a book.

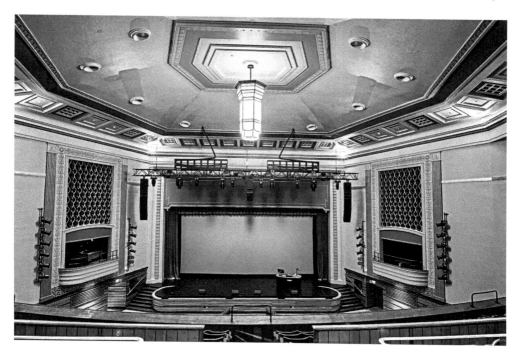

The People's Palace auditorium.

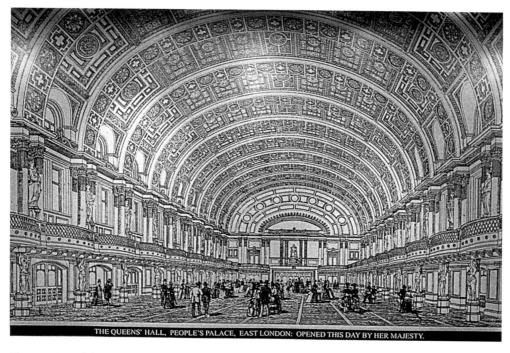

THE QUEENS' HALL, PEOPLE'S PALACE, EAST LONDON: OPENED THIS DAY BY HER MAJESTY.

The opening of the Great Hall, People's Palace, in 1887. (Courtesy of Queen Mary University London Archives)

Inside the Palace is an Art Deco delight. Created by cinema designer George Coles, the stairwell and meeting halls are restrained in décor so as not to detract from the activities planned to take place there. People came from all over London to hear concerts, opera, meetings and public events, and film shows. In 1954, the Palace was incorporated into the college to be used for exams and seminars and renamed the Queens' Building in 1956, but recent renovations include new signage proclaiming the original name of People's Palace.

The long-forgotten Octagon also gained a new lease of life. Having been left in a state of general decay, a restoration programme in the early 2000s included improved acoustics, cleaned paintwork, patching up the leaky roof and adding solar panels in the lantern. In 2011 it was reopened, to be used regularly for exams, open days and seminars, but the public are always welcome to visit when it is not in use.

## DID YOU KNOW?

# Four Queens

The Queens' Building is now named for four different Queens, hence the apostrophe after the 's'. Queen Victoria opened it, Queen Mary granted the Royal Charter, Queen Elizabeth the Queen Mother was Chancellor, and Queen Elizabeth II is currently Patron.

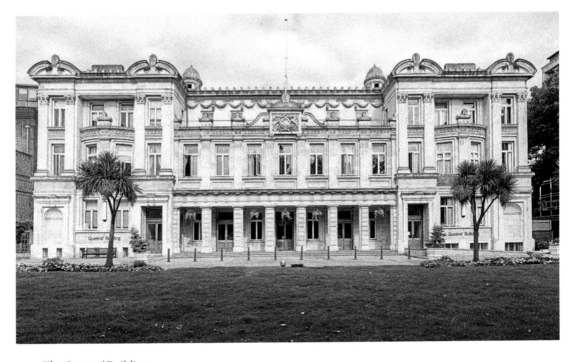

The Queens' Building.

# About the Authors

## Louis Berk

A photographer and teacher, Louis Berk's work has been published in newspapers, magazines and books on subjects as diverse as Banksy and the 'Boris Bus'. He has previously published *Walk to Work* (2008), a four-year photographic project set in Whitechapel and Spitalfields, *School Work* (2010), a unique insight into an inner-city secondary school and *Ampthill* (2012), an architectural perspective on a group of tower blocks in North London. His first two books for Amberley Publishing were *Whitechapel in 50 Buildings* (2016), co-authored with Rachel Kolsky, and *East End Jewish Cemeteries: Brady Street and Alderney Road* (2017), a five-year photographic study of two historic Jewish cemeteries. You can find out more about his books and photographs at louisberk.com.

## Rachel Kolsky

Rachel Kolsky is a prize-winning London Blue Badge Tourist Guide who is passionate about exploring London's heritage. Her walks and talks cover a wide range of themes and areas but always focus on the 'human stories behind the buildings'. Her first book, *Jewish London* (2012), was co-written with Roslyn Rawson and her second, *Whitechapel in 50 Buildings* (2016) with Louis Berk. When not guiding or writing, she can be found speaking as a guest lecturer on cruise ships or in her local independent cinema, where she was a trustee for over twenty years. You can find out more about her walks and talks at golondontours.com.

# Acknowledgements

The authors would like to thank the following people and organisations for permission to use copyright material in this book: Sharon Allin; Mychael Barratt; Bishopsgate Institute; Keith Bowler; Ronnie Cohen; Stefan Dickers at Bishopsgate Institute Library; T. V. Edwards; Marta Esteban at Dennis Severs' House; Freedom Press; Gentle Author and his Spitalfields Life blog; Melvyn Hartog at the United Synagogue Burial Office; Lutfun Hussain; Stuart Kira; the quotation from Journey Through a Small Planet, by kind permission of the Estate of Emanuel Litvinoff; Rupert Marquand at Queen Mary University London; Barry Musikant at S&P Sephardi; Miriam Phelan at the Jewish Museum; Kevin Pooley and Steven Spencer at the Salvation Army International Heritage Centre; Ivan Reback; Jennifer Rinkoff; Ray Rinkoff; Royal London Hospital Museum; Richard Watts; Mhairi Weir at Spitalfields City Farm and the team at Amberley Publishing for their assistance and guidance.

Every attempt has been made to seek permission for copyright material used in this book; however, if we have inadvertently used copyright material without permission/ acknowledgement we apologise and we will make the necessary correction at the first opportunity.

All photographs are the copyright of Louis Berk unless otherwise stated.

# Locations

Please check websites for public access before visiting.

Introduction. T.V. Edwards, 33 Mile End Road, E1 4TP; tube: Whitechapel
1. Bishopsgate Library, 230 Bishopsgate, EC2M 4QH; tube: Liverpool Street. bishopsgate.org.uk
2. Dennis Severs' House, 18 Folgate Street, E1 6BX; tube: Liverpool Street, Shoreditch High Street. dennissevershouse.co.uk
3. Artillery Passage, E1 7LJ; tube: Liverpool Street
4. Crispin Street, E1 6HQ; tube: Liverpool Street
5. David Kira, 1 Fournier Street, E1 6QE; tube: Liverpool Street
6. Leyden Street, E1 7LE; tube: Aldgate
7. Merchant House, Wentworth Street, E1 7TS; tube: Aldgate East
8. Rothschild Arch, Wentworth Street, E1 7SA; tube: Aldgate East
9. 19 Princelet Street, E1 6QH; tube: Aldgate East, Liverpool Street. 19princeletstreet.org.uk
10. Christ Church Primary School, 47a Brick Lane, E1 6PU; tube: Aldgate East
11. Several sites throughout Spitalfields – see entry for details
12. London Recording Studios, 9–13 Osborn Street, E1 6TD tube: Aldgate East
13. Altab Ali Park, Whitechapel Road, E1 1FD; tube: Aldgate East
13a. St Boniface, 47 Adler Street, E1 1EE; tube: Aldgate East
14. Angel Alley, E1 7RA; tube: Aldgate East
14a. Jewish Daily Post, 88 Whitechapel Road, E1 7QX; tube: Aldgate East
15. Several sites throughout Whitechapel – see entry for details
16. Pedley Street Arch, E1 5ES; overground: Shoreditch High Street
17. Spitalfields City Farm, Buxton Street, E1 5AR; tube: Whitechapel. spitalfieldscityfarm.org
18. Bearsted and Ada Lewis Courts, Underwood Road, E1 5AW; tube: Whitechapel
19. Montefiore Centre, Hanbury Street, E1 5HZ; tube: Whitechapel
20. Vallance Gardens, Vallance Road, E1 5BG; tube: Whitechapel
21. Fulbourne Street, E1 5AA; tube: Whitechapel
22. LARC, 62 Fieldgate Street, E1 1ET; tube: Whitechapel. larcwhitechapel.wixsite.com/larc/
23. Whitechapel Road, E1 1ES; tube: Whitechapel
24. Royal London Hospital, Whitechapel Road, E1 1BB; tube: Whitechapel / The Royal London Hospital Museum, St Augustine with St Philip's Church, Newark Street,

Whitechapel, E1 2AA; tube: Whitechapel. bartshealth.nhs.uk/the-royal-london-hospital-museum-and-archives

25. Royal London Hospital, Stepney Way outside Cavell Entrance; tube: Whitechapel

26. 259 Whitechapel Road, E1 1DB; tube: Whitechapel

27. Alderney Road Jewish Cemetery, Alderney Road, E1 4EG; tube: Stepney Green / Brady Street Jewish Cemetery, Brady Street, E1 5DW; tube: Whitechapel. theus.org.uk/burial

28. 23 New Road, E1 1HE; tube: Whitechapel

29. Tommy Flowers Centre, 16 Henriques Street, E1 1NB; tube: Aldgate East;

30. St George's Mortuary, 14 Cannon Street Road, E1 0BH; tube: Shadwell

31. Peter House, 279 Commercial Road, E1 2PS / Painter House, 1 Sidney Street, E1 2HU / Siege House, Siege House, Sidney Street E1 2HQ – All tube: Whitechapel / City of London Police Museum, Guildhall, 2 Aldermanbury, EC2V 7HH; tube: Bank. cityoflondon.police.uk/about-us/history/museum

32. Erlich Cottages, Sidney Street, E1 2EL; tube: Whitechapel

33. Rinkoff's Bakery, O'Leary Square, 222–226 Jubilee Street, E1 3BS; tube: Whitechapel Rinkoff's Café, 79 Vallance Road, E1 5BS; tube: Whitechapel. rinkoffbakery.co.uk

33a. Brick Lane Beigel Bake, 159 Brick Lane, E1 6SB; overground: Shoreditch High Street

34. Grove Dwellings, Adelina Grove, E1 3AE and several sites throughout Whitechapel – see entry for details

35. Dunstan Houses, Stepney Green, E1 3JH; tube: Stepney Green

35a. 4 Stepney Green, E1 3JU; tube: Stepney Green

36. Belle Vue Place, E1 4UG; tube: Stepney Green / Mile End Place, E1 4BH; tube: Stepney Green

36a. Tower Hamlets Mission, 31 Mile End Road, E1 4TP; tube: Stepney Green, Whitechapel. towerhamletsmission.org

37. Velho and Nuevo Cemeteries, Queen Mary University of London, Mile End Road, E1 4NS; tube: Mile End. sephardi.org.uk

38. Queen Mary University of London, Mile End Road, E1 4NS; tube: Mile End. qmul.ac.uk. To visit the People's Palace or Octagon check with Reception, Queens' Building

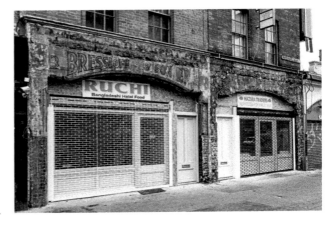

An old shop sign revealed during renovations on Whitechapel Road in 2014. As Whitechapel continues its transformation the sign has once again been covered over.